Unbreakable

Other Titles by This Author

RISE: The 8 Keys to Overcoming Adversity and Living a Life You'll Love

The RISE Journal: A Simple Way to be Happier and Have More Peace

Average to AmaZing: The Young Leader's Guide to a Remarkably Resilient and Happier Life

(recommended audience: elementary students)

Unbreakable

9 Steps to a Life of Joy,

Strength and Purpose

Kwesi Millington

Disclaimer. The events and conversations in this book have been set down to the best of the author's ability, although some names and details have been changed to protect the privacy of individuals.

First paperback edition September 2024
First eBook edition September 2024

Book design by Victoria Barclay
Book cover by Sandro Parisotto

ISBN: 978-0-9959278-5-8

Published by the author.
https://kwesimillington.com/

DEDICATION

Quite simply, this book is dedicated to you –
the young leader, the world changer,
the resilient and confident you.

The words I write are delivered
with one purpose:
to help you live the best and fullest life
possible.

Thank you for inspiring me to give
all that I have.

CONTENTS

Introduction

Unbreakable...it's what I teach students to become...in my writing and in my speaking. But I have something to confess. NO ONE is unbreakable. You and I have been broken at times, and there will be more times when you are broken, mentally and spiritually. (You're probably thinking, "You're a motivational speaker, Kwesi? That's not very motivational!")

But here's the good news: every broken moment is a chance for you to grow stronger. You may not feel it when you've been knocked down, but when you rise up from the pain, the hurt, the hopelessness.... it's the person you become in the process that is more unbreakable than the one who originally stumbled.

However, it's not an automatic process. There are definitely steps you can take – simple to remember – that can help you become the strongest, most confident version of yourself. The YOU that can get through anything. The YOU that shines when others stumble. The YOU that turns pain into purpose. I've written this to help you do just that. But first...

Can I share a letter I've written? It's a letter to my younger self. It's what I'd say if I sat face to face with the little boy from Montreal, Canada. The boy who was picked on, bullied, and uncomfortable in his own skin. As you read it, see if any of it resonates with you. Because I'm writing it to you as well. And if you want to talk to me about anything you read in the letter, or any part of this book, write me at kwesi@kwesimillington.com.

LETTER TO A YOUNGER ME

Dear Kwesi,

First things first. Let me tell you this: I love you. And I'm proud of you. Not for anything you've done. Not for anything you've accomplished or created. Just because... I know your heart. I know your thoughts. I know that you think that you need to be great at something. I know you think you have to make a certain impression to be worthy. I know you think you have to be liked and noticed by certain people to feel important. But you don't. Your worth was established from birth. From the moment you were born, you were worthy. From the moment you were born, you were enough. Stop trying so hard to show the world you matter. You already do.

But I know sometimes you don't believe any of this.

That teacher...he told you your work was garbage. So you started to think that you needed the approval of others. Those kids who made fun of your shoes ... they said your sneakers looked old and cheap. So you started to think that the way you looked and what you wore determined your value. That lady on the plane who changed seats when she saw you...you went home and looked in the mirror. You started to think that your skin color was ugly. You just wanted to fit in. You just wanted to be ... different. And you ARE... but that's a good thing.

Remember that show you used to watch? The Transformers? Well, what would that show be like if EVERY robot was Optimus Prime? Or Bumblebee? Or Megatron? Pretty boring, eh? You were meant to be different. You were meant to express your unique self to the world – not for more friends, more popularity, or more…anything. But simply because you are SUPPOSED to be you. And I know it's hard. This world will tell you that fitting in and being the best are your most important goals. But here's the only goal that I want you to focus on: being – and accepting – who you are, no matter if anyone else does.

Will you feel lonely at times? Yes. Will you feel the pressure to change? Absolutely. But stay true to you. Why? Well let me tell you where we are now. The (much) older version of you has some wisdom to share…

Those differences you hated about yourself? Some people spend a lot of money trying to replicate your darker skin and full features. Those people who made fun of you? I don't remember most of their names, or even their faces. Those people who didn't accept you? I can't find them anywhere – the people in my life now couldn't care less what shoes I wear or how much money I have. There are people that will like – and love – you for you. But the most important person that has to love you, to care about you, to accept you… is you. There are many things I could tell you to do, but I'll just leave you with one …

Go to the mirror every day and night and repeat this statement: "YOU ARE POWERFUL. YOU ARE BEAUTIFUL. YOU ARE PRICELESS. AND NO MATTER WHAT… I ADMIRE YOU, AND I ACCEPT YOU JUST THE WAY YOU ARE."

Say those words, young one, because that's exactly how I feel about you. I LOVE YOU.

Kwesi

AND YOU...

I love to read. I didn't always love it, but the journeys and wisdom of others has helped me survive some of the lowest moments of my life. I truly hope that you enjoy reading this book. We're going on a journey through my life, a journey that I hope will help you to reflect on yours. And as you read, make notes, directly in this book if you feel like it. And feel free to take pictures of the words that you connect with, and the ones you write too (If the mood strikes, share them online and tag me too @KwesiSpeaks – all social).

But most of all, use these words to help you to believe in yourself, to believe in your dreams, and to build the hope that no matter what you *go* through, you can *grow* through. Let's begin our journey together to #becomingunbreakable.

PART I -- HOW YOU THINK

Chapter 1

Reframe Your Reality

Whatever we focus on is bound to expand. Where we see the negative, we call forth more negative. And where we see the positive, we call forth more positive.

– *Marianne Williamson*

THE CRAYON

If you look up the word "unbreakable" in the dictionary, you'll read that it simply means "unable to be broken." That definition is misleading. It gives the impression that to be unbreakable, you are like Superman – invincible and incapable of being hurt. If you go by that meaning, then when things go wrong, when you feel down or depressed, you'll wonder if that makes you weak. You may think that being broken means that you are not as strong or as capable as someone else. That is the furthest thing from the truth. A moment with my son taught me that.

Toddlers wear their emotions on their sleeves. They display them loud and clear at all times. It can be very cute. It is often quite frustrating. For example, my son Phoenix once experienced the life-altering tragedy of dropping his crayon on the ground and watching it break. He was three years old when this happened, so you might be able to imagine the pool of tears and echoing screams this caused.

As soon as the crayon bounces into two pieces on the floor, his beautiful brown eyes look at mine and his tears flow immediately. “It’s broken, Daddy! I can’t use it anymore!”

I look at him and gently reply, “Yes, we can. We can still use the pieces.”

He persists: “NO! It’s broken!” Then he picks up the pieces and starts walking towards the kitchen garbage.

I see the teaching moment clearly. I take the two pieces, one in each hand, and kneel down next to him.

"Phoenix," I say softly.

"Yes, Daddy?" he replies through sniffles.

"Does this piece still color?" I give him one of the broken crayon pieces and direct his hand to the abandoned *Paw Patrol* coloring book.

He hesitates, then colors one of the pictures (not within the lines, of course!). As he does that, he replies, "Yes..."

I continue, taking the remaining piece in my hand and coloring on the page. (Red, even though the puppy named Chase is supposed to be blue. I'm grateful Phoenix doesn't focus on that inconsistency.) Then I ask, "Does *my* piece color too?"

"Yes, Daddy!"

"Then that means we can BOTH color now, right?" I smile.

So does he. "Yes, Daddy! Let's color together!"

A moment of sobs and sadness returned to happiness and play for my son. The reason is simple: I showed him that broken can still produce beautiful. Read that again: BROKEN CAN STILL PRODUCE BEAUTIFUL.

Just because you've been broken, hurt or disheartened by life, doesn't mean your brokenness is permanent. Just like that crayon, you can break and still bounce back. You can suffer and still soar. You can be broken, and still create a beautiful life. *That* is what the word *unbreakable* means to me. Now let's look at how photo albums help you to reframe how you look at things…

THE PHOTO ALBUM

"Does anyone even have a photo album anymore?"

I was having a conversation with a friend, and he asked me that. The question made sense. Most people store all their photos on their phones or online these days. Apps like Facebook and VSCO (and likely more by the time you read this book) make it easy to revisit your memories on a screen. There is no need to print pictures anymore.

But call me old-fashioned. I like printing photos. I still like the feeling of a real picture. Putting it on my desk. Hanging it on a wall. Putting it in a frame...and every once in a while, changing that frame. There's something about re-framing a picture that gives it new life. It's like I look at the photo differently, with new eyes. I've learned that life works the same way.

Finding a way to change how you look at your circumstances often gives you the energy and motivation to find a way to cope and overcome. Your ability to look at things differently can only benefit you. Just like there is more than one exercise that builds strong legs, there is more than one way to look at basically anything in life. Fail a test? You can look at it as a reason to drop the course, or a reason to double down on your study time. Lose a friend? You can look at it as proof that people can't be trusted and put your guard up. However, I've found that sometimes a "friend" who leaves your life wasn't meant to be in your life in the first place.

Going through a personal struggle? You can look at it as a reason to grow negative and pessimistic about life. You can look at it and think life sucks. You have every right to do that at times. I don't know you, but I honor the fact that sometimes you may hurt. Sometimes you may feel alone. Sometimes you may feel the deepest of pain. But I know that sometimes those personal struggles teach you how NOT to be. Let me give an example.

THE TWO CRIBS

My mother and father split up when I was very young. Let me explain why…

Mom used to be a nurse. While she was pregnant with me, something happened that changed our lives forever.

She walked into her Montreal townhouse and saw something on the counter when she entered her kitchen: a receipt for a baby crib. Now you might be thinking, "*Kwesi, she's pregnant…a baby crib receipt makes sense…*" But here's the thing:

Mom already had a crib for her first and only child. That receipt… was for a second crib.

Remember a time when you were caught “red-handed”? When you were busted doing something you shouldn’t be? You know that face of guilt that you couldn’t hide no matter how hard you tried? (Or the face of guilt on the person you caught?)

Well, that was Dad’s face when Mom showed him that receipt. Faced with no other option, he admitted that not only was he having an affair, but he was about to have a child with another woman. Boooooo…

Soon after I was born, my mother and I left my father, and moved to Toronto where she would raise me on her own. I saw my father a handful of times growing up (he died when I was twenty…more on that story later), but part-time parenting is never an adequate replacement. And I noticed.

My best friend had his dad in his life, and there were times I resented it. When you see another dad playing video games with *his* son, coaching *his* soccer games, and generally just…being there…it hurts.

But fast forward a few decades, and not having an ever-present father taught me a valuable lesson: It taught me how NOT to be.

Pain breeds opportunity. Being bullied gives you the opportunity to be a loving, kind person, because the pain of being picked on reminds you that you would never wish that feeling on someone else. Having a friend betray you gives you the opportunity to be an even better friend to those who truly value you. And for me, having a part-time dad reminded me that I never want my son (who was three years old at the time of this writing) to feel the absence of the most important male role model a young boy can have.

So the question is: how do you teach yourself to look at things differently? In other words, how do you train your "reframing" muscle? We'll get to that soon, but first, let me share a mistake I made due to lacking that "male role model."

WHAT *NOT* TO DO WITH YOUR PAIN

Ian has been my best friend for over thirty years. We've been through a lot. We're both parents now and don't see each other as often as we used to, but that's how life goes. I don't think I've slept over at anyone's house as much as his while I was growing up. And there's one thing I remember vividly about the times at his place – the presence of his father. Going home to no man in the house was not something I noticed when I came home from school or piano practice, but it was definitely felt after coming home from Ian's place. The pain was real. The jealousy was too. And I handled it poorly on one day in particular.

Ian and I both loved video games growing up. He was a fan of the company Sega; I was a Nintendo kid. But we both enjoyed marathon sessions playing whatever game we decided on. One day, I was with Ian at a video game store. He picked up a new game with what I thought was a hefty price tag at the time. He took it to the counter and paid for it. As we walked out of the store, I thought, "I wonder what Ian's dad would think of his son paying that much for a video game!" So as soon as we all reunited at our predetermined meeting point in the mall, I told him. I ran up to Ian's dad right away and said, "Do you know what Ian just paid for that game?" and I exposed the price paid.

I smirked at Ian. Ian looked at me with a mix of surprise and disgust. His dad looked indifferent. What I didn't realize is that Ian's dad gave him the money for the game…the price was no surprise to him. I also didn't realize why I did that…why I felt the need to "snitch" on Ian to his dad. I was too young at the time to understand the reason was simple: I was trying to transfer my pain.

Ever since my dad and mom split, I've felt a void. A lack of a father in my home. Hey, my mother is amazing – she did everything for me and I couldn't have asked for a better one. But you can't help but feel a sense of rejection when your father moves thousands of miles away (from Canada to Trinidad) and leaves you behind. And here's what I know: there are consequences to avoiding or suppressing your pain. Pain is energy – it doesn't just dissolve. It MUST go somewhere. And on that day in the mall with Ian, it came out in an ugly way.

Here's the truth I've come to realize about that day: I was trying to make Ian's dad feel negatively toward him. I was trying to make Ian feel some of the rejection that I felt from my father's absence. I was trying to make his father dislike his son. That's messed up on so many levels. In fact, now that I think of it, I owe Ian another apology for that day. Sure, we were just boys then. Sure, I was misdirecting my pain. But I was an ass, and Ian would have had every right to disown me after that day. I didn't know what to do with my pain, so I tried to give it to someone else.

Remember, pain is energy. It is a feeling that must be addressed, or it will manifest in other ways. It's why people commit crimes based on jealousy. It's why some students choose to bully others. It's why some adults do it too. If you've ever been treated negatively, chances are it has nothing to do with you. It's them. It's that person's ignored or suppressed pain coming out in another form.

Don't try to push down your pain.

THE TOILET PAPER RULE

I have a personal question for you: What direction do you put the toilet paper on the roll at home? Are you an "over" person or "under"? (Unimportant fact: The patent for toilet paper was developed in 1891 and the correct way to put the roll on according to the patent is with the sheets flowing over the roll, not under.)

Now another question for you: Have you ever been to the house of someone who had the toilet paper roll on the opposite direction than you're used to? Did you change the direction? (Or did you want to?)

The reason I ask that is because we get used to things done a certain way. We get up in the morning, go through the same routine, and then go about our day. If you look back at the last week of your life, chances are it's not much different than this week. There's nothing wrong with that – routine is good – in fact, essential – to maintaining a sense of balance and good mental health. However, studies have shown that even though routine is a good thing, inserting small changes every so often into that routine trains your brain to look at things in different ways.

Why is that a good thing? Because your ability to reframe a negative situation to see the positive that you can take from it is a key to being resilient throughout your life. I call it "finding the gift."

Back to the "pain is energy" thing... when you think of hurt you've experienced, ask yourself "Can I flip the way I look at this?" Just like you put the toilet paper on the roll the same way every time, as humans we tend to look at and treat our pain in a repeated pattern. Our reactions become habitual, and if we never stop and try to look at things differently, we go through life without ever changing or growing. Reframing the way you approach the tough times in life allows you to find what I call the "possibility of positivity."

Here's a challenge for you: change something that you do daily. Start with something small, like changing the direction of your toilet paper rolls at home. (Your family will love that!) Other options include walking a different route to the store or school, re-arranging your room, etc. These seemingly insignificant practices will train your brain to say: "How can I look at this differently?" The "toilet paper rule," as I call it, will help you build resilience. So, the next time you go to the bathroom, think of this section of the book. (Weird thing to say, I know!)

ANOTHER REFRAMING STRATEGY

When I speak to students, many will often ask me: "Kwesi, how did you get into motivational speaking?" My answer: Les Brown and Toastmasters. The year 2013 was a year of transition. I had started a new relationship, moved to a new house, and, due to my lengthy perjury trial, was looking at the possibility of having to start a new career outside of policing. Needless to say, there was a lot of change, a lot of stress – and a lot of tears.

Not many people saw me cry, but I would spend many afternoons out for a drive, feeling hopeless, and crying as I listened to motivational speeches on YouTube. Sometimes the tears were due to thinking about all the uncertainties of my life, and sometimes they were simply due to the combination of motivational words and uplifting music combined by Goalcast and other skilled online video-mashers. The bottom line is this: I was looking for inspiration. I was looking for someone to help me forget my problems and feelings of worthlessness. I was looking…for someone to give me hope, direction and motivation. Then I found Les Brown.

Les Brown was born in 1945 in Liberty City, a poor section of Miami, Florida. His mother couldn't afford to raise him, so she put him up for adoption. He faced ridicule and judgment, even being labeled as "educable mentally retarded" in grade school. Despite a rough childhood, he would eventually popularize the saying "Don't let someone else's opinion of you become your reality" – advice given to him by one of his teachers. Brown would eventually go on to become one of the most successful and popular motivational speakers in the world. His voice can not only be heard in his speeches, but in countless motivational audio mash-ups on YouTube, which is where I first heard him.

According to Steven Southwick, former psychology professor and co-author of *Resilience: The Science of Mastering Life's Greatest Challenges*, one of the key factors in building strong mental health is to find resilient role models to learn from and imitate. Les Brown became that for me. Here was someone who rose above his circumstances and now gives the world hope, courage, and motivation through his words. Something in me awoke whenever I would hear him. A small voice inside me said, "Use *your* words to spread hope, too." So, when I heard Brown mention the organization called Toastmasters, I was intrigued.

Toastmasters is a worldwide organization, founded in 1924 by Ralph Smedley with the purpose of helping people develop their communication and leadership skills. There are 145 countries around the world that have over 16,200 such clubs. In 2013, I joined a local Toastmasters club. My improvement wasn't instantaneous, but I started to learn how to speak more effectively. I hired coaches. I then became a Certified World Class Speaking Coach in 2015. And I use the skills I've learned from Toastmasters, coaches, and the best speakers in the world to become a professional speaker myself. At the time of this writing, I've spoken to students, teachers, and organizations from all over the world, providing hope, inspiration, and motivation. And it all started with words spoken by Les Brown.

One of the best ways to reframe your own pain is to seek out and find mentors who have reframed theirs. Find those who have turned their struggles into strategies, strength, and personal success. Whether you meet them online, live – or just through books, audio, or video – find people who have risen above their pain and found purpose.

The next key to becoming unbreakable that we'll encounter in Chapter 2 lies in two words: letting go.

UNBREAKABLE BLUEPRINT:

REFRAME

Before we start with these end-of-chapter reflections, please do this: take the time to write down your answers. Countless studies have shown that what you write down has more mental permanence and relevance than that which you simply think about. Thinking is great; thinking *and* writing is even better. The following questions are designed to help you turn the words you've read into the unbreakable life you can create and live.

#1 – Think of your "broken crayon" moment. Has there been a time that you've felt broken but were still able to do or achieve something? Has there been a circumstance in your life that, though negative, you were able to take something positive from? Outline it. Remember it. Your past stories are a reminder of the strength you already possess.

#2 – What is something that you can change in your everyday routine? It can be as simple as switching the toilet paper roll. Whatever it is, remember that the small changes you make in life will make you more mentally flexible and resilient to handle bigger changes that you will inevitably encounter.

#3 – Find a role model who has gone through struggle or had something they've overcome in their life. Whether it's through a book, documentary, or video – search for people who have demonstrated resilience in their lives. Find one person this week and write down three ways that they have demonstrated mental strength. The more you do this, the less alone you'll feel when you go through pain in your life, and the more confidence you'll have that you can rise above anything.

PHRASES TO REMEMBER

You have full permission to repost anything you resonate with… just tag me @KwesiSpeaks!

The Broken Crayon Rule – Broken can still produce beautiful.

The Two Cribs Rule – You can't choose your reality, but you can choose your response.

The Toilet Paper Rule – Courage comes from change and curiosity.

Chapter 2

Release Your Need for Perfection

If I'm going to live at peace, I've got to surrender my expectation of perfection.

– *Steven Furtick*

THE SOCIAL MEDIA "BLURSE"

Social media can be many things. I call it a "blurse": a mix between a blessing and a curse.

I don't want to vilify social media, but the statistics don't lie. A survey by the National Center for Health Research uncovered the following facts:

- The rate of adolescents with depression increased by 52 percent from 2005 to 2017
- Students in Grade 8 who spend over 10 hours on social media weekly are 56 percent more likely to report being unhappy

- Spending more than three hours on social media daily leads to a higher risk for mental health problems
- Reducing social media use to a maximum of 30 minutes per day resulted in lower levels of anxiety, depression, loneliness, and sleep problems.

Using social media activates the brain's reward center by releasing dopamine, a "feel-good" chemical linked to pleasurable activities. But the mental health and confidence issues have simply not made the dopamine rush worth it.

What is really happening when people go online? Let's look at that…

Social media has created a society of empty cups. What do I mean by that? When you are thirsty, you take your empty cup, fill it with something to drink, then empty it again. The cup is always waiting to be refilled. Most people are the same. They are always hungering for more to feel satisfied: more likes, more friends, more attention. When they get the attention they crave, the cup is full – until they see someone whose picture or video received more praise. Empty cup. I heard the comedian Chris Rock say on one of his specials that our biggest addiction is attention. He's right: deprive someone of food, they will hold out for a few days – or at least a few hours. But take away their cell phone – pandemonium! That's because most people use that device to feed their attention addiction.

Maybe what I've described isn't you. Maybe you're not addicted to attention and you use the force of social media for good. Regardless of what group you're in, you know that can be true too: social media can be used for good. Movements are created. Connections are formed. People use it to "find their tribe" and feel less alone. There are pros and cons for sure. However, there's one thing I know for sure: no one can be on any social media outlet for too long without feeling at least slightly insecure, imperfect, or inadequate.

My full story is explained in the book I'm most known for, *RISE: The 8 Keys to Overcoming Adversity and Living a Life You'll Love*, and in later chapters of this book, you'll learn parts of it as well. When I spent time in solitary confinement, I was forced to have time away from the outside world. I consider solitary confinement a "blurse" in some ways. The blessing of such seclusion is that I didn't have my electronic handcuffs (a.k.a. my iPhone) with me. I left behind my family. I left behind my home. But here's what else I left behind: comparison. I wasn't comparing myself to my next-door neighbor with the bigger house, to the ripped trainer online, or my friends' vacation trips. There was no one's attention to chase and no one chasing mine. I felt invisible. And at times that was an absolute feeling of freedom.

When I regained my freedom, it was like walking out of a pitch-dark room after 24 hours into the brightest day. Except instead of the rush being beautiful sunlight, the rush was the demands and distractions from the outside world. All of a sudden, I was connected again. Was it a blessing to have freedom and connection to my family and friends? Absolutely. But I was also re-connected to everyone I knew online, and how much everyone was doing in my absence. I felt like the world had left me behind and everyone was doing so much better than I was. And I only spent ten months in the correctional system. I can't imagine how someone must feel after ten years!

I know my expectations weren't realistic. I know that I needed to give myself grace – I was starting over, after all. But it didn't stop me from feeling like a loser: a failure. I spent years trying to become a police officer, only to have it all end, leaving me with nothing. And when you already feel like a failure, going on social media doesn't do much to reverse that feeling of inferiority. Failure has a tendency to destroy confidence, but not because of the failure itself. It destroys confidence because of what most people do *after* failing.

A Grade 1 failure taught me that lesson.

THE SPELLING BEE

I wasn't the best student, but for some reason I have always been a pretty good speller. Give me a word and most of the times I could visualize and spell it correctly. I wasn't *Scripps Spelling Bee* international competition material, but I was better than most – so I thought. And that ability took me to the finals of the class spelling bee in Grade 1.

Picture the scene: a class of around 30 students, all competing. Our teacher, Mrs. K, gives word after word, and child after child is eliminated. Round after round results in more and more desk seats being filled and the row of standing students decreasing. Finally, the competition comes down to two young and eager students.

You can probably guess who one of them was…the other was a girl that I'll nickname "Sweet Sarah." I call her sweet because she had cute little pigtails, always looked perfectly dressed, and was generally a nice little girl. She and I were very different students, even at that young an age. She was already very social; I was a shy, introverted kid. I started reading later than other kids – a decision that my mother reached when she saw my cousin who was a year younger than me reading before I could. At the age of four, I still couldn't read, so my wonderful mother started doubling down and reading to me even more regularly so that I wouldn't be behind when I started school. That extra attention made a difference. I caught up with my reading, and exposure to all those words allowed me to become a good speller too. Hence, I outlasted a class of students to get to the finals of that Grade 1 spelling bee.

Mrs. K gives us our final word: ALWAYS. I get the first chance to spell it. Full of confidence I take a step forward and loudly say the word followed by the spelling of each letter:

"Always. A – L – L – W – A – Y – S. Always." I smile. I look at Mrs. K. She is *not* smiling.

She reports the result with a sombre voice: "Kwesi, I'm sorry but that is wrong."

I'm shocked – I could have sworn I spelled the word correctly! I didn't look, but I'm sure some of the other students were smirking. *They* knew that I mistakenly added the extra "L."

And unfortunately for me, so did Sarah. She spells the word correctly: "A – L – W – A – Y – S."

Mrs. K congratulates her and awards her the prize – a pack of pencil crayons. I sit down and put my head down on the desk, tears of shame and embarrassment fill my eyes.

Memorial lanterns are often used as a ceremonial way to remember those who have passed away. Also called sky lanterns, they are released into the sky at a memorial event, allowing attendees to celebrate a loved one and provide some closure. We ought to do something similar – even if in our imaginations – about our failures. When we falter or fail at something, we should symbolically place the memory of that failure in a sky lantern or balloon, let it float away, and move forward with our lives. Unfortunately, most people never do that. They hang on to the memory, letting it deflate their confidence, produce limiting self-talk, and fill them with self-doubt. Unfortunately, that's exactly what I did.

If you had been in my classes back then, you would have seen a kid who went from taking chances, to a kid who was always holding back. You would have seen a young boy who let his shyness take over, sitting further and further to the back of the class until it was like he was invisible. That was me: no raising my hand in class, no speaking up – and *definitely* no more spelling bees!

There's an old saying: "No risk, no reward" – meaning that if you don't take chances, you'll never know what your potential reward could be. I wasn't worried about that. I simply thought, "Kwesi, if you never put yourself out there, then no one will ever know how *stupid* you are ever again!"

Harsh, right? Was I *really* stupid for losing a Grade 1 spelling bee? Of course not...but that didn't stop me from calling myself stupid – and worse. I internalized so many negative voices growing up. Some were self-inflicted, others were from fellow students – and unfortunately, some were from a few teachers. Whether from myself or others, I internalized everything negative I experienced or heard from others and became my own worst enemy.

Have you ever talked down to yourself? Ever let a temporary failure or insult become your permanent mindset? Have you internalized voices of negativity, leaving you feeling incomplete, invisible, or invaluable? If so, here's what to do about it, starting TODAY.

It's something you may have heard of, and I learned it from a trip to Mexico.

A BURGER AND A BOOK

As a reward for graduating from Toronto Metropolitan University (when I attended it was called Ryerson University), I decided to join my brother for a getaway trip to Mexico. We landed in Cancun, ready for sun, surf, sand... and – to be transparent – girls!

But first, we checked in to our hotel, then hopped on the local bus to head downtown for some food. I love to eat, and one thing I enjoy when traveling to different countries is trying local cuisine (as long as I trust the restaurant!). As much as I love Taco Bell, I was ready for some authentic burritos, tacos, and homemade guacamole! So, when we got off the bus on that busy downtown

Cancun street, I was looking around for a Mexican restaurant – and then I saw something totally unexpected.

Have you ever looked at someone and thought: "Why would you do that?" Well, my brother and I got off the bus and we saw the most popular restaurant in downtown Cancun. The place was packed – with both locals and tourists – and then I saw him. A guy came out of the restaurant and took a bite ... out of a BIG MAC!

Yup, McDonald's was the most popular restaurant on the downtown strip! Now, that may not be surprising to you – after all, you can find a McDonald's in almost every country in the world. However, I looked at some of the *tourists* coming out with fast food and thought: "Why would you do that?" Why have a burger that you can get in your hometown, when you have the opportunity to sample a country's local cuisine? It wasn't until I got back home to Canada and read a book that I realized why McDonald's and other fast-food restaurants remain just as popular abroad as they are at home. The book is called *What to Say When You Talk to Your Self* by Dr. Shad Helmstetter.

Dr. Helmstetter holds a Ph.D. in psychology and is a best-selling author. He has appeared on national television multiple times and has been a guest expert on one of the most popular talk shows of all time, *The Oprah Winfrey Show*. When I read his most famous book, *What to Say When You Talk to Your Self*, one line stood out to me over all the others: "The brain simply believes what you tell it most."

When I read that, I realized immediately why McDonald's was the most popular restaurant in Cancun. The reason is quite simply because they told us they are popular and should be our top choice for food when we're hungry. How does McDonald's do this? By spending hundreds of millions of dollars in advertising each year. And that's just a fraction of the BILLIONS spent by all fast-food companies in worldwide advertising on an annual basis. Now why does this advertising work? Because of a feel-good hormone called dopamine. Enter quick science lesson...

Dopamine is a neurotransmitter made in the body that makes us feel good. It allows you to feel pleasure, satisfaction, and motivation. That's a simplistic definition – which makes sense, because I'm not a doctor or scientist. Here's what's important to remember: there's a part of your brain called the dorsal striatum that releases dopamine when you see an advertisement or smell fast food.

All consummatory action (for example, buying or eating something) comes first from a feeling. Remember that: it all starts with how you feel. So when you see the McDonald's commercial or billboard, your dorsal striatum says, "Hey, let's release some dopamine!"

The dopamine makes you feel hungry and crave the burger. Then, regardless of the fact that you *know* McDonald's food isn't the healthiest option, your feelings take over and you end up in the lineup. And your brain makes a connection: Eating a Big Mac = Feeling Good. Whether you say it out loud or not, your brain gravitates to what it's been exposed to and told the most. That's why that Mexican McDonald's restaurant was packed. It's also why a spelling bee led to my complete lack of confidence.

Humans are predictable – they like to chase good feelings and run from bad ones. If something makes you feel good, you will likely repeat the behavior. That goes for both positive and negative behaviors. For some, working out feels good, so they repeat the activity. For others, the feel-good activity is eating, which has led to record levels of obesity in North America. Either way, we chase good feelings. However, the flip side is also true. When you have a bad feeling, you will often do whatever it takes to make sure you don't feel that again. In Grade 1, I lost in a spelling bee. I was embarrassed. I felt like a loser. My brain made the connection like a voice in my head: "You lost that spelling bee, Kwesi. Didn't that feel horrible? Don't ever put yourself out there like that again!" So I didn't. I let a temporary failure turn into a permanent mindset. Have you ever done that? If so, here's the mistake we both made: we forgot that failure is an inevitable toll to pay on the road to success. Look at any successful person, and you'll learn the absolute truth of that statement. However, that doesn't take away the fear of failing, or the temptation to quit – or not even try.

What helps counteract that? A term that you may have heard of before: self-talk.

MAKING YOUR BRAIN WORK FOR YOU

Remember what Dr. Helmstetter said in his book: "The brain simply believes what you tell it most."

I want you to focus on one word in that statement: YOU. Your brain believes YOU. Your brain will follow what YOU tell it to do, think and believe. It doesn't matter if it's a McDonald's commercial, something someone says to you, or the voices you've told yourself when you fail. YOU have the power to override anything you've seen, heard, or experienced. YOU have the choice: let your failures define you or speak new power into your life.

There's a Bible proverb that says: "The tongue can bring death or life." (Proverbs 18:21 NLT) That's the weight that your words have: they can figuratively bring you death or life. There are people who have put themselves down, both internally and externally, for decades. They speak negative or self-defeating words and go through their lives wondering why things never "work out" for them.

Conversely, there are those people who have CHOSEN to speak positively, regardless of their circumstances. They speak words of belief and self-worth. Their self-talk is positive, and their life aligns with their words. Now this doesn't mean they don't experience struggle, pain, or hardships. They have simply decided that they are not going to add to their *external* circumstances with negative *internal* dialog. No matter what has happened to you in your life, you have the power to at least change your thoughts about what has happened. Remember this acronym: AFTER.

(A) Actions, flow from

(F) Feelings, which flow from

(T) Thoughts, which flow from

(E) Expectations or beliefs you've developed, which flow from

(R) Registered programming, namely, the words you've said to yourself or believed from others.

This process is easy to apply to hunger. You ate the burger (action) because you were hungry (feeling), which came from the idea that fast food was what you wanted to eat today (thought), which flowed from the belief you had that the burger tasted great in the past (expectation), which is a result of the advertising that you have been previously exposed to (registered programming).

This process can be applied to ANY action you have taken or will ever take.

This should excite you, because that means that if you start with R – Registered Programming – you can start to control your actions, and change your life.

So, what is "registered programming"? Think of it like a cash register. If you purchased a new one and didn't put any money in, then when you open it what would come out? Nothing. You have to put money in (the program), in order to get it out. If the "register" is your brain, how do you program it? Through your senses: sight, smell, sound, touch, and taste.

Let's start with two of those senses: sight and sound.

If your brain believes what you tell it the most, why not tell it what *you* want it to believe? Doesn't that seem so simple? It is, but it's not easy. There are two reasons that most people never do this: Belief and Discipline. Some people don't believe that they can change their life by changing the words they use. Science proves that you can.

This brings us to the second reason that many people never use self-talk to improve their self-esteem – they don't make it a habit. Think of your favorite food. Do you know how many times you've seen it advertised in your life? Neither do I. I have no idea how many fast-food commercials or billboards I've seen in my life, but I know they have worked. Maybe not the first time, nor the tenth...but they did eventually work.

The same goes with confidence self-programming – you don't know how many times you'll need to speak and/or write empowering words to yourself. But don't think of it that way. Just make it a regular habit, because ongoing self-talk will benefit you for the rest of your life. Just like putting cash into the register, writing, speaking, and visualizing yourself as successful and confident will make you mentally stronger and emotionally powerful. Now let's look at how you can start doing it today.

HOW TO MAKE SELF-TALK A HABIT

Here's an exercise to help you become the person you want to be: Go somewhere where you won't be disturbed. Sit down and close your eyes (after reading all these instructions). Imagine the ideal version of yourself. Engage as many senses as possible. What do you see, feel, and hear? Paint a specific picture in your mind. For example, before I deliver a speech, I close my eyes and imagine myself walking up on stage, feeling confident and walking tall. I paint a mental picture of myself speaking. That cancels out any fearful thoughts such as forgetting part of the speech or being nervous.

Whenever you want to change a situation or circumstance in your favor, begin the process by painting a picture of what you want in your mind – even if you don't believe it yet. Start in your imagination and your thoughts, feelings – and eventually your life – will follow.

Once you've done the visualization exercise, get out a pen and paper. Write down the words "I am." Then think of two or three words that describe the person you just visualized. Write each word after each "I am." For example, you could write:

"I am confident!"

"I am brave!"

"I am beautiful!"

Or whatever words come to mind. Now this is a longer process to use, but you can do this quickly by simply taking out a post-it note, writing "I am…" and your words on it and repeating them to yourself throughout the day. Keep the note with you and repeat the words when you feel anxious or less than your best. By keeping reminders of the *words you want to feel* handy at all times, you'll be more likely to make positive self-talk a habit.

Another way to use self-talk effectively is by using it immediately after you have a self-defeating thought. This requires you to be present and realize when you are beating yourself up, but if you can, in that moment, write down the negative thought in the form of a conversation. For example, if I feel ugly, I might write: "I look so floppy and ugly right now. I'm looking old and tired."

I often tell the young people that I speak to that *you have to recognize it to release it*. By recognizing the negative self-talk, it makes it easier in the moment to release and rewrite the thought to become more empowering.

For my example, I would cross out the words I wrote (preferably in a different color to make it stand out), and simply write the opposite: "I look great. I don't judge myself for how I look. I feel great and my age is bringing wisdom that I didn't have when I was younger. I get smarter, wiser, and better every day!"

I want you to notice the new self-talk that I wrote. Notice it wasn't unrealistic. I didn't write, "I look like a bodybuilder." I simply wrote a gentler, *more compassionate* version of my original self-talk. I urge you to do the same. One way I've found to bring more presence into this practice and get more regular with my self-talk is to keep a journal handy. The human brain likes to stick with what is easy. If you always have a journal and pen with you, you're much more likely to remember to recognize your negative self-talk and re-write your positive words of self-empowerment. By having that journal with you, you are telling your brain:

"See? I made it easy for you to record your thoughts and self-talk! Now keep up the habit!"

So what's next? Read on for how to deal with those things that are out of your control. See you soon, my friend!

UNBREAKABLE BLUEPRINT:

RELEASE

Since you have a journal, let's outline your answers to the following to help you release the need for perfection. If you don't have a journal yet go out NOW and grab one from your local dollar store!

#1 – Write down the ways you've been comparing yourself to people you see online or in real life. Is your perception realistic or have you set unreal expectations for yourself? Are you setting yourself up for inevitable low self-worth with who you follow and interact with? Remember, it's okay to take a break from anything or anyone that makes you feel invisible or invaluable. (At the time of this writing, I have just taken a self-imposed one-month break from social media for my mental health.)

#2 – Have you ever had a "spelling bee" moment? A time when you let a temporary misery turn into a long-lasting or maybe even permanent mindset? Do this: write down the details of the event, then – with a different colored pen – write down the positive aspects of the moment, what you learned, and something that you can take from the moment. For example, in my spelling bee, yes I lost, but I outlasted 28 other students to make it to the final two. I learned that just because you fail, doesn't mean you should never try again. What can you take from your situation?

#3 – Write down five to ten self-talk statements that describe the actions you want to take or the person you want to be. For example, if you want to start a workout plan, you could write: "I am motivated to go for a daily run/workout. I get up with energy and drive to exercise." If you just want to write down feeling words, just do that. (For example: "I am confident. I am beautiful.") Next, put these statements in three places where you cannot miss reading them every day. Good areas include: your journal, your bathroom mirror, your bedside table. Remember that you think thousands of thoughts per day. It's going to take a commitment to self-talk to make your mind work for you instead of against you!

PHRASES TO REMEMBER

Repost away, and I'd love for you to tag me @KwesiSpeaks!

The Social Media Rule – Take a break from anything that makes you feel broken.

The Spelling Bee Rule – Don't turn a temporary misery into a permanent mindset.

The Self-Talk Rule – The most important words are the ones you tell yourself.

Chapter 3

Relinquish Your Uncontrollables

History cannot be unlived.

– *Maya Angelou*

OCTOBER 14, 2007

If you haven't read my first book, *RISE: The 8 Keys to Overcoming Adversity and Living a Life You'll Love*, you may not know my full story. You can watch a short video at https://bit.ly/resilienceinterview, but I'll give you a synopsis here, extracted from *RISE.* (If you know my story, feel free to skip this section.)

There are only a few careers where "Lunch Time" can be at one o'clock in the morning. Policing is one of them. When the call came in that would forever change my life, I thought I was in a good place. I had a career I loved, in a unit that was rarely busy. I liked that. I wasn't an "action junkie" cop. When the high-speed chase was on, I went for backup out of duty, not desire. The call that many police officers hate – the family dispute "counselor" call – was the one I used to love.

That's why, when years later a lawyer looked right at me in court and said, "I bet you couldn't wait to use your Taser, could you," I had to laugh a bit inside. That lawyer had *no idea* what a peace-loving cop I was. I was thinking, "If you only knew me! If you only knew that I was bullied twice in my youth, making me detest all forms of bullying! Those types of statements are so alien to who I am that it's laughable."

Nevertheless, you can read stories and articles about what happened on the night of October 14, 2007, at Vancouver International Airport in Canada. You will pick up the basic overview. A man, now identified as Robert Dziekanski, was reported throwing luggage around an airport. Four police officers from the Royal Canadian Mounted Police (RCMP) responded to the call. One used a Taser (that was me), and Dziekanski was placed under arrest. At some point soon after that, his heart stopped. There is no absolute proof as to the cause of death, but the opinions are numerous.

Some people accuse me of electrocuting him to death with my Taser. That's an opinion.

Some people accuse the four of us of using excessive force that caused him to die. That's an opinion.

Some people, including some doctors, say that he had a pre-existing medical condition based on his profuse sweating and agitation when we encountered him, and that as soon as he was arrested, *regardless of method*, he was doomed to die. That, though it is a statement to the benefit of me and the other three officers, is also just an opinion.

There are many OPINIONS about what happened that night, but here are the FACTS. Robert Dziekanski arrived on a flight from Poland to be picked up by his mother. For reasons unknown, he started to damage airport property, including attempted destruction of electronics and furniture. At that point, we (three other officers and I) were called to intervene. After seeing the man on the secure side of the airport terminal, we attempted to communicate with him. The language barrier prevented proper communication. The man picked up and opened a stapler, and started to advance towards us. I pulled out and used my Taser, and we handcuffed and arrested him. He started to go into cardiac arrest soon after. Despite intervention by firemen and ambulance attendants, he died.

I had heard that when police officers have to intervene, tragedy can result. However, just like a death in the family, you are never prepared for when it happens to you. I knew we had to apprehend and restrain Robert Dziekanski that night, but I never thought in a million years that he would die. And even though I was told that happens in our job, and though I was reassured that any other officer in my place would have acted the same way, I couldn't help but think about the events of that night and wonder if anything could have ended differently.

When a situation moves quickly, and the outcome is unexpected, it's easy to analyze and play out imaginary alternate endings. I had only one reality. The truth.

The TRUTH is that we did our jobs. A tragedy resulted, but we did what we were trained to do.

The TRUTH is that the events of that night were recorded.

The TRUTH is that we all gave statements outlining what happened that night.

The TRUTH is that a report was given by an RCMP officer on national television outlining the events, WITHOUT anyone contacting us or reviewing our statements beforehand.

The TRUTH is that when the public saw the video AFTER hearing the incorrect reporting of the events, there was an outcry for something to be done about "the cover up of the truth."

The TRUTH is that there was a public inquiry into the events of that night in October. I testified on March 2-4, 2009, at the Braidwood Inquiry, and to be honest, I was looking forward to FINALLY getting my side of the story out and achieving vindication.

The TRUTH is that the judge overseeing the inquiry wrote a scathing report afterwards, accusing us (the four officers involved) of many things, most notably of exaggerating our statements in October in order to make our actions appear justified and Mr. Dziekanski's actions appear worse than they were.

The TRUTH is that I had previously been cleared of any wrongdoing by prosecutors in British Columbia, Canada, as well as by the RCMP, and was quite transparent with my statements and testimony at the inquiry.

The TRUTH is that for whatever reason, a Special Prosecutor was subsequently allowed to review the details of the case and was given carte blanche to charge any or all four of us with a criminal offense. This, despite the clearing of our names previously.

The TRUTH was that in 2011, I was charged with Perjury (lying under oath with intent to mislead), for statements made at the Public Inquiry. An inquiry that I later found out was not mandatory that I participate in.

Nevertheless, I was convicted in February 2015 and sentenced to 30 months imprisonment in June 2015. I would eventually start a prison sentence on October 31, 2017. I spent ten months in the Canadian Correctional system for perjury, a crime I did not commit.

And don't just take MY word for it: a best-selling book was written by an award-winning investigative journalist from the CBC (Canadian Broadcasting Corporation) outlining the entire case. I am eternally grateful to Curt Petrovich, the author of *Blamed and Broken: The Mounties and the Death of Robert Dziekanski*. His book clearly indicates that the perjury charge was baseless and should have never been approved. In addition to that, as of

2025, I am eligible for a complete pardon from the charge and conviction, which will wipe it completely from my record.

A HATEFUL RESPONSE

When I speak to students, I don't share everything that you just read. I speak about the perjury charge, yes. I also speak about resilience lessons learned in prison and from being wrongfully convicted. However, if you are a student who has ever heard me speak, you would have never heard the airport taser story. That's not because I'm ashamed of sharing it with you, but simply because I've been asked by many school administrators to leave that part of my story out. Do students google me before or after listening to me? ALL THE TIME. And, if asked, I explain the honest and full truth. But I leave the full story up to the individual student to investigate on their own.

I tell you this because I've had many principals and school administrators flat out say, "We will not be bringing you in to speak to our school due to your story." Those are the nice ones. Some have simply ghosted my request, and a couple of teachers have said much worse. I have been getting hateful, racist emails and messages sent to me for years. The good news is, I'm kind of immune to the online keyboard cowards at this point.

Is a hateful email a worse response than either ghosting or a school simply deciding that they don't want to risk bringing me in due to my story? The answer is yes. But what I've learned is that you can never control someone else's actions or opinions. The only thing you have complete control over is *your* opinions, *your* words, and *your* actions.

If you haven't run into it yet, you will – people who don't agree with you, don't like you... or flat out hate you. You may have been bullied. You may have been hurt. You may have your haters. Remember that you cannot control *their* decisions, only *your* actions.

As mentioned in the previous chapter, it's vital to release not only the need for perfection but also the things in your life that you have no control over and the people who have made a decision about you – fair or unfair. From personal experience, I know that when you try to change situations, thoughts, or opinions about your circumstances, it only leads to pain, regret, and wasted energy.

Oh, you know by now there's a story behind this one! Let me tell you about a time I made an ABSOLUTE fool of myself trying to get back at someone...

THE FIRST FIRING

I've been fired twice in my life in a very memorable way. The first time happened when I graduated from university, got a job... then was "let go." It's always hurtful to the ego to be fired, but when I look back, what you're about to read taught me an important life lesson that would help me when I was fired for a second time.

Let's not get ahead of ourselves, though...

In my early twenties, I was working in a temporary position for the Ontario government. An opportunity arose for me to settle into a permanent role in the office, doing similar work to what I was already doing, so I jumped at the chance. I applied for the role, figuring that I was a lock to get it. After all, my manager was happy with my work, and I felt confident with everything I had been asked to do. But (there's always a "but," isn't there?) the problem was this: the manager responsible for the hiring for the permanent position was *not* my manager.

Have you ever met someone and immediately gotten the vibe: "I don't think they like me"? Whether it was a look, the tone of their voice when they talk to you, or some other clue, I believe we inherently know if we're going to get along with someone or not. Yes, there are times when that first impression turns out to be way off, but many times you just know. Well… that was the relationship I had with the manager responsible for the hiring of that permanent position. We rarely spoke to each other, and when we would walk by each other in the office, let's just say, "If looks could kill…" Okay, maybe it wasn't that bad, but I could definitely tell that I wasn't her favorite person. And unfortunately… that was the person who held my hopes for that permanent job in her hands. I think you can guess how this story ended.

I sat down in her office, with a big oak desk between us, and she did not take long to get to the point. I'm sure she said many things during that last meeting, but this is what I remember clearly:

"Kwesi, you didn't get the job – and we WON'T be keeping you here."

Have you ever remembered EXACTLY what someone said to you when they put you down or said something negative? Those were her exact words…and that was that. I walked out of her office – and the building – for the last time.

Or so I thought.

Fast forward three years, and I'm in Regina, Saskatchewan. It's May 16, 2005, and I have graduated, becoming a police officer with the RCMP. I'll never forget when they put that gold badge in my hand for the first time. Regimental number: 52147

– that's the distinguishing number I received as my unique identifier. It was beautiful! I showed my mom the badge. I flew back to Toronto and show my friends the badge. If I was out on a date – yup – I even showed the unfortunate lady across from me my shiny new badge!

I was so proud...and immature. Speaking of immaturity, guess who I wanted to show that badge to? Yup, the woman from that government office who fired me. I wanted her to know that she knocked me down, but now I'm back up and have an even better job! You're probably thinking "But Kwesi, it's been THREE years! Weren't you over that firing? Move on!" I should have. But I didn't. Before I flew from Toronto to Vancouver for my first days on the street (my first policing posting was in the city of Richmond which is just outside of Vancouver, British Columbia), I went right back to that government office to brag!

I remember the day – and the moment – that changed how I would look at resentment forever. I walked back into that government office, found my old manager, and asked him almost immediately if the woman who fired me was working that day. He looked at me pensively, then told me that unfortunately, she wasn't at the same office anymore. She got a promotion, and he hadn't been in contact with her. And then he said it – three words that I'll always remember: "She moved on."

Have you ever been instantly embarrassed by your behavior? Nelson Mandela, former president of South Africa and winner of the Nobel Peace Prize, once said that when we hold grudges, it's like drinking poison, hoping it will kill our enemies. The poison of resentment only hurts the person holding the grudge.

At that moment in my old office, a phrase came to me that I often tell both students and adults in my role as a Professional Resilience Speaker: *You can't move forward, when you're looking back*. I was holding a grudge against someone who not only had moved on, but likely didn't remember firing me in the first place!

Is there someone or something that YOU can't let go of or are holding resentment towards?

Stop drinking the poison. Move forward. Let it go.

I'll talk about how to do that a bit later, but first let me tell you how the firing and my immature response actually *helped* me when I got fired for the second time.

DECEMBER 12, 2017

In the autumn of 2017, I was still in solitary confinement when I received a visitor. There was a knock on the thick metal door and the guard uttered two words: "Millington. Visitor."

I was escorted to the prison library and sat across from a well-dressed middle-aged man in a suit. I recognized him as a high-ranking officer of the RCMP. Besides the fact that we were both members at the time ("members" is the term the RCMP often uses instead of "officers"), we couldn't have looked more opposite. I was wearing the standard issue "blues" – blue jeans and a blue shirt. There's some irony here: "blues" is the term for the pants you wear as a trainee at the RCMP academy in Regina, Saskatchewan, before you earn the right to wear an upgraded version closer to your graduation. I went from pre-officer blues, to prison blues (pun intended). So here I am in prison blue clothing, with dry skin and a face that hadn't seen a shave in weeks. I guess this officer – who has seen me before – couldn't think of anything better to say, so he just said this:

"You don't look too bad!"

In that moment, I felt insulted by the comment. Looking back, however, I believe he was just trying his best to navigate an awkward situation. I don't remember much else about that conversation, except the strange comment, and his forewarning me that I would soon be discharged from the RCMP (another word for fired). He sympathized with the fact that I was unjustifiably convicted of perjury but mentioned that there was a rule within the RCMP that if an officer has served jail time after a conviction, they cannot remain employed by the Force.

Thus a few weeks later, on December 12, the warden's call was no surprise.

I walk into a boardroom and sit down at a table. It's designed to seat around twenty people, but today there are only four: myself and three well-dressed officers from the RCMP. The words are a blur; the reason for the meeting is crystal clear. Sign here, goodbye, thank you for your service. After twelve years, that was my last day as a police officer.

Getting fired is a strange thing. Even though many times the person can sense the inevitable, it still hurts. Maybe it's the finality of it all. Perhaps it's just the blow to the ego and my pride. As Maya Angelou once said, "People will forget what you said, but people will never forget how you made them feel." So true. I don't remember one word that was said to me during that meeting, but even as I write this, I remember the feeling. Loss, sadness, hurt. I needed to talk to someone, but not those men in the room. I headed to the prisoner phone area (located in the laundry "house" in the prison) to call my wife Cindy.

Once again, the words she exchanged with me are not what I remember. What I do recall was that my tears soaked the sock on the payphone handset. (Hundreds of prisoners use the same phone, so most inmates covered the handset with their own sock before using it to prevent the spread of germs.)

Unexpected events trigger strong emotions, but I had prepared myself for the eventuality that I would be fired. I knew it was coming, so why did I cry? There are likely many reasons, but I believe one of them is that there was now no hope at all that I would continue my career as an officer. There's an old saying that humans can live three *days* without water, three *minutes* without air, but not even three *seconds* without hope. Obviously, this is not exactly true, but hope *is* that important. And when it's snatched away for the final time, it hurts – deeply.

So, what do you do when life takes those unexpected turns? What do you do when you feel hopeless? How do you let go of who you were or what has happened to you, in order to become what you're meant to be?

I reflected on this once I finished that phone call with my wife. I believe that when you take silent time to reflect – and even write down your thoughts – answers seem to come to you as if by magic. What I know now is that your best answers, thoughts, and ideas will *always* come to you when you take some silent time to yourself to reflect and ask the right questions. And the question I asked myself was: where do I go from here?

HOW TO LET GO OF YOUR PAST

Reflecting on my future, I asked myself, "What have I done in the past when life took an unexpected turn?"

The answer came almost as soon as I asked: You can't move forward when you're looking back… *so keep looking forward*!

Remember that first firing in that government office? Well, even though I did eventually go back and try to find the manager who fired me, what got me past that resentment – at least temporarily – was focusing on a future goal. That goal was to become a police officer. And even though I indulged my immaturity by trying to hunt down the woman who fired me, the focus on, and the accomplishment of, my goal is what allowed me to move forward.

Is there something you're holding on to? If so, it can be like what happened to Tobey Maguire in the 2007 movie *Spider-Man 3*. In the movie, Maguire's version of Peter Parker (I'm not going to argue who is the best Spider-Man of all time, but.... Tom Holland gets my vote!) accidentally takes home an alien goo called a symbiote. If you've ever seen the black-suited Spider-Man, that's what happened when Parker let his bitterness about the past – including the death of his Uncle Ben – affect him and his personality. The symbiote fed off Parker's anger and resentment, eventually attaching itself to his suit. This dramatically enhanced his powers, but also his aggression, anger, and other negative qualities. Parker was eventually able to rid himself of the symbiote, which found another host in Eddie Brock – an even angrier and more aggressive person – and the infamous character Venom was created.

Resentment, anger, and bitterness about the past is like that symbiote. It attaches itself to your personality, and at times it may feel good to swim in those emotions. However, long term, the result can only hurt and frustrate you. I'm not telling you that you have to forget your past, but I am saying that looking forward and setting new goals and sights for your future will ease the hold that your past has over you. When people ask me how I was able to let go of any bitterness towards the RCMP and the Canadian justice system for the situation I found myself in, I credit focusing on my future for allowing me to release my "resentment symbiote." Becoming a motivational speaker and certified coach has helped me along that path.

If there is something that you find hard to let go of, ask yourself this one question: "What is something that I can look forward to?"

HOW TO PLAN FOR YOUR FUTURE

Years ago, I went to a live seminar led by motivational speaker Tony Robbins. I took a lot out of that experience, but one thing he said really stuck with me, maybe because of what I had personally experienced in my own life. He said that the best way to get over your past is to focus on your future.

As I look back at those last few years of my policing career – being involved in a major tragedy, accused of lying about it, then going to prison for perjury – I reflect on what allowed me to move from policing to professional speaking. It came down to the truth within Robbins' quote. In order to thrive through tragedy, survive setbacks and break through your breakdowns, you MUST be willing to look forward and plan for your future.

When I stayed mentally stuck in the misery of my imprisonment, I experienced nothing but depression and a spirit of defeat. The switch came when I started to journal and meditate on what my new future could look like. Focusing on what the future *could* look like – even if the picture was still unclear – gave me new hope, new energy, and best of all, lifted me out of the depths of despair. That's the key to remember – you don't have to have a clear vision of the future to be positive about what the days, weeks and months ahead will bring. You don't have to know all the answers. Just be willing to ask the question: "What could my future look like?"

Keeping a vision on the road ahead will help you to stop doing what most people do too much of – staring in the rearview mirror. A good friend of mine once told me: "Kwesi, there's a reason the rearview mirror is so much smaller than the windshield. You're supposed to be looking forward."

YOUR THREE-STEP PROCESS FOR GOAL SETTING

If you ask ten people to detail their goal setting process, you'll likely get ten different answers. Sure, you'll see commonalities, but everyone approaches planning their future in a slightly different way.

However, from what I've seen of the hundreds of systems for productivity and achievement, there are three steps that keep coming up as keys to not only setting goals but also achieving them. I've found the steps you are about to read essential to adopt when planning your future. Let's break them down to help you apply them in your life.

STEP #1 – WRITE YOUR FUTURE

There is something empowering about writing out your future. Do this: pretend you are one year into the future. Write out all the things you've accomplished over that year as if it has already happened. For example, don't write, "I will lose 10 pounds." Instead, write, "I have lost 10 pounds."

Choose a date – it doesn't have to be exactly one year away – and now write your future with the phrase "It is (future date), and I'm so happy that I… (your future)."

Or you could write, "As of (future date), I am/have (future accomplishments as if already accomplished)."

Write your future out in complete detail. When you do, ensure that you include all the areas that mean the most to you, such as your finances, fitness, faith, etc. Write it as if you are already living the end result.

STEP #2 – KEEP IT VISIBLE

Once you've written out your ideal future (typically this exercise is about a page in length), keep it in a place where you can see it often. The best places to make sure this stays visible are the ones that you have to be in or see for other reasons, such as the bathroom, the screen saver on your laptop, or on your phone.

Wherever you place it, keep it visible so that you can remember your goals and vision daily. Human rights activist Malcolm X once stated: "The future belongs to those who prepare for it today." Keeping your goals visible is preparing you to walk into your future life.

STEP #3 – SEE IT HAPPENING

Albert Einstein, considered to be one of the smartest people to have ever lived, once said:

"Imagination is more important than knowledge." Here is a man who craved knowledge, and was very "book smart," but still valued the power of imagination. There is a limit to knowledge. Your imagination is unlimited.

So here's the last step to your goal-setting process: *imagine* it happening.

Imagination can affect your reality. Here's proof of that. In 1996 a study was conducted at the University of Chicago on the power of visualization. A group of randomly selected students were asked to shoot a series of basketball free-throws. The percentage of successful free throws were scored, then the students were divided into three groups. Each group was asked to perform a separate task over a 30-day period:

- Group #1 did nothing.
- Group #2 was asked to practice free throws every day for 60 minutes.
- Group #3 was asked to close their eyes, and simply *visualize* themselves making successful free throws. They did this every day.

The results were surprising.

- Group #1 showed no improvement (no surprise there!)
- Group #2 showed a 24 percent improvement.
- Group #3 (the group that only visualized successful free throws) showed a 23 percent improvement in real life!

The study results were astonishing and proved beyond doubt that visualizing directly affects your reality. Now let's put this superpower to work!

The visualization process is simple: spend a couple of minutes every day away from any distraction. Close your eyes and literally "see" yourself having accomplished your goals. If your goal is to live on a waterfront property, close your eyes and see yourself sitting on your dock, hearing the waves lapping up against the rocks, feeling the warm cup of coffee or tea in your hand as you relax into your day.

Want to own a certain car? Go to the dealership and sit in it. Observe everything you can about it.

Then once a day, sit in silence for a few minutes and re-live the feeling of the contoured seat, the smell of the leather interior, the smooth ride as you drive on the highway (going the speed limit of course!).

Whatever your goal happens to be, write it, keep it visible, and use your imagination to live in that future. Now, let's finish the chapter with practical tools to help you accomplish those goals.

MANAGING YOUR TIME

When I conduct student personal development workshops, one of the main questions I get asked is: "I have my goals, but I can't seem to manage my time effectively to get it all done!"

This is not surprising. Most people spend far too much time doing low-to-no-value activities. YouTube rabbit holes, anyone? I once read that the average person checks their phone 96 times per day! Is it any wonder that we find it hard to get things done?

Do you have a system to manage your time? If the answer is no, don't feel bad – most people don't. As with goal setting, you can easily google "time management systems" and come up with lots of options. Let me share with you what I share with students in my workshops. I call it "The 5-B System."

B1 - BUILD

I don't remember who said it to me, but I'll always remember the words: What doesn't get scheduled, doesn't get done. An easy way to stop putting something off is to **build** it into your schedule. Putting everything I do into my calendar ensures that I get to everything that needs to be done in a given day.

When planning your schedule, start by working backwards from your long-term goals. For example, start by breaking your one-year goal down into what needs to be accomplished this month to get there. Then **build** the smaller tasks in, step by step.

B2 – BEGIN

Have you ever put off a task that you just didn't want to do? You know the feeling – you wake up in the morning with one major task to do, but by the time you go to bed you've been "busy," but that "one thing" never got done.

How do you feel when that happens? You probably feel unfulfilled, because even when you get a lot of things done, you really wanted to cross that major task off your list.

Conversely, isn't it a great feeling when you stop procrastinating and get it done?

Here's how to make sure you always have that feeling: **begin with the biggest bite**. Simply start each day with your most important goal. Whether it's something you've been putting off, or the task that will lead to the biggest results in your life, tackle that as your first goal every day.

Putting off working out? **Begin** your day at the gym.

Need to finish a major assignment you've been dreading? **Begin** your work dedicated to that.

Hate making calls for a job or your business? **Begin** with your calls before you do anything else for the day.

Begin with the task you've put off or need to do the most, and your day will be much more productive and meaningful.

B3 – BURSTS

Studies have proven that breaking down your work into timed sessions helps to overcome a lack of self-discipline and builds motivation to get things done. Methods such as the *Pomodoro technique*, developed by Francesco Cirillo, have made this step – setting timers for your tasks – a popular productivity hack.

When Cirillo was a university student, he found that he couldn't focus on getting his work done. So he did something that changed his life – and the lives of countless others since: he grabbed a tomato.

Wait, what?!?

Okay, specifically, he grabbed a tomato-shaped timer and set a 10-minute timer. After a 10-minute **burst** of focused work, he took a short break. Discovering that using these shorter, timed **bursts** of work made him much more productive, he called the method the Pomodoro Technique: "pomodoro" being the Italian word for tomato.

If you ever feel unmotivated to get something done, set a timer, do a **burst** of work until it rings, then take a short break.

How much time should you set your timer for? The general consensus seems to be anywhere between 25 to 50 minutes before taking a break, but experiment and do what works for you.

B4 – BRIEF

Enter the next problem that many people run into. The dreaded to-do list. Setting a list of tasks to accomplish in your day is a good tool to use. However, making that list impossibly long turns a positive tool into a disempowering one. I used to set to-do lists that never got completed. Sure, I got things done, but I started to feel like every day was an impossible mission, and there were times I felt totally deflated.

Then one day I sat down and predicted the time needed to actually complete my list. The result was eye-opening: I would need *two to three* days to complete everything on my one-day list! Most people overestimate what they can get done in a day, the result being a feeling of overwhelm and disappointment.

Avoid this by setting a **brief** to-do list. Be honest with yourself: can you *really* get more than 3 or 4 quality tasks done in a day? Most people think they can do more than they think they can. They end up multitasking themselves into confusion.

Before you create it, make sure that your to-do list can be completed in the time you have in one day. Sometimes, I like to add some “extra to-do’s” – tasks that I can tackle if I finish my main list. With the word “extra” added to these items, I am telling myself that they are not “musts” for the day. That way, when I reach the end of my day, I feel I’ve accomplished something, whether or not I get to these items. Remember, there's always tomorrow. Keep your to-do list **brief**.

B5 – BONUS

Here's one more way to help you manage your time effectively that I learned on vacation. On a family trip to Jamaica, I remember sitting at the buffet eating a fried bake. Well, the actual name is "Jamaican Festival Dumpling." As I bit into my fifth dumpling (yes, I gained a bit of weight on that trip), a resort employee walked over, and with a warm island smile looked at me and asked in his lovely accent, "Yuh know what makes that taste so nice?"

Mouth full, I didn't answer, but my eyes indicated to him that I wanted to know.

"Suga!" he said.

The secret ingredient was to sweeten the dumpling with sugar. The sugar acts as a **bonus** to the tastebuds.

Use that same approach with the tasks you don't want to do: give yourself a **bonus**. How? By coupling the task you are procrastinating on, with some kind of reward.

Do you love watching online videos but hate writing English essays? Do this: set a 25-minute timer to work on the essay, then a 15-minute timer to watch videos as a **bonus**.

You'll be both focused on the work you need to get done *and* be motivated to get to your entertainment **bonus**. You're rewarding the work you must do, by coupling it with a **bonus** that you enjoy.

Sometimes you might even be able to combine them. For example, if you need to get in your 10,000 steps, but also want to finish that book you're reading on Audible, go for a walk while you listen. Combine your "have-to's" with your "want-to's" and you'll be that much more motivated and productive.

UNBREAKABLE BLUEPRINT:

RELINQUISH

#1 – Think of a situation you are worried about. Make a list of everything that concerns you about this situation. Really take your time and ask yourself what makes you anxious or worried about it. Now... circle all the items on that list that are within your control to change. For most people, there are just a few. What you will likely find is that most of what you worry about is out of your control.

#2 – Ask around and find someone who has gone through a similar situation to yours. You may find this through asking friends, reading about someone online, or in a book. Find out what they did to let go of their past, then duplicate their efforts. Success leaves clues, and I promise that someone out there has gone through the same struggle that you have and has offered advice about how to relinquish resentment, guilt, shame, pain, or other negative feelings.

#3 – Write down one or two goals that you have for the future. They can be physical, financial, educational or any other category that you choose. Make sure that you're motivated by the goal, then choose one thing you can do today or this week that will move you closer to that goal. When you focus on your future, the past loosens its hold upon you.

PHRASES TO REMEMBER

Repost away, and I'd love for you to tag me @KwesiSpeaks!

The Rearview Rule – You can't move forward when you're looking back.

The Double Handcuff Rule – What you hold on to, is holding on to you.

The Goal-Setting Rule – Put away your past by focusing on your future.

PART II -- HOW YOU FEEL

Chapter 4

Reach Out for Help

Life is too difficult to navigate alone.

– *Dr. Jordan Peterson*

THE QUIET PAIN

My mother is not a very emotional person, so it surprised me when I saw her tear up during my trial for perjury. For most of the days she attended, she sat stoically, silent, and strong. But on this day, she started to cry. During the break, I asked, "Mom, why are you crying?"

She simply said, "Because I wish you had told me you had been bullied."

What you're about to read is what my lawyer summarized and conveyed during my trial.

In Grade 2 I was bullied by a boy named Bobby. I was a skinny kid and didn't have many friends which made me an easy target. I think I blocked out much of what went on between us, but here is what I remember. I lived less than ten minutes away from Highfield Junior School in Rexdale, a Toronto neighborhood. Rexdale is home to many immigrant families, and diverse in culture. The apartment we lived in was not well-maintained, and we shared occupancy with more cockroaches than I could count. Fortunately, my mother and I moved when I was in Grade 3.

They say you don't know what you don't know, and since none of my friends were much better off than I was, it never bothered me that we didn't have a lot of money. I walked to school, and most days I was pretty happy. However, when Bobby targeted me, school days quickly became a scene out of a suspenseful action movie that I didn't want to be in.

Most days went something like this: I would walk to school, hoping not to see Bobby on the way. Every time the bell went off, I was on high alert.

"Will he spot me walking the halls?"

"Can I get to my next class without him seeing me?"

"Do I have to go outside for lunch?"

"Can I leave a few minutes early at the end of school so he won't notice me?"

Some days I got lucky. Now "lucky" didn't always mean that I didn't see Bobby. Bullies are like employees: sometimes they take days off. There were days that he would punch or shove me anytime he'd see me, and others when he would ignore me completely (the lucky days). The problem was that I never knew which version of Bobby I'd get, so I was always hypervigilant. If you had measured my cortisol levels (the stress hormone) during those days, it would have been through the roof! But somehow, I always hoped that there would be a "last day" of bullying. Maybe, I thought, he'd get tired of bullying – or at least bullying ME. And one day, I thought that moment had come.

I'm riding my bike home from school; the hope being that if I can hop on as soon as school is finished, I'll be gone before my tormentor could notice. No luck, however. A few blocks away from the school I look ahead and see Bobby walking with another boy on the sidewalk ahead of me. Before I can turn around, he looks back and spots me.

"Hey, Kwesi!" His voice sounds calm. Perhaps it's a day off today.

I sheepishly reply, "Hey, Bobby." As I approach him, I slow down, but do not stop. I ride on the grass as I pass him.

"See ya," he says.

"See ya," I mirror back.

Phew! I think. *At least today is a bully-free day!* I veer back onto the sidewalk, speed up, and start to turn the corner at the end of the block. Metaphorically, I believe we are "turning the corner" in our relationship too. The end of our toxic, bullying mess of a relationship. I am wrong.

I feel a sharp, sudden pain in my right arm. It's so shocking that I lose my grip as I turn the corner, tumble off my bike, and roll onto the grass. *What was that?* I think.

The mystery doesn't last long. There's a rock on the ground next to me. I hear two boys laughing behind me. One laugh is far too familiar. It's Bobby. He'd thrown a rock with deadly accuracy as I rounded the corner. The rock hit its mark – my shoulder – knocking me to the ground. I guess we *haven't* turned the corner in our abusive relationship. He walks by me, laughing as I nurse my bruised shoulder. I wait until he walks far enough to be out of eyesight. Then I allow the tears to flow.

Childhood had happy moments for me, but that was one of my saddest. If you've ever been bullied, I want you to remember this: *only broken people try to break other people*. Something that I didn't understand back then is that there are always reasons that people bully, and 99.9 percent of the time they have NOTHING to do with you. You may just remind them of the issues they are dealing with, or bullying might just be a pattern they've seen or a misguided way of handling their inner pain. Of course, some people ARE just plain mean, but for the most part there is a deeper reason behind their behavior.

School can be a lonely place. A place for nourishing relationships and self-actualization for some, it can be a source of deep pain and an initiation to life-long trauma for others. What I've learned is that if the latter is the case for you, the worst thing you can do is bottle up and hide your pain. All feelings are energy and will come out anyway (more on this later), so the best thing you can do is to find someone to reach out to when you feel alone, ostracized, or broken inside.

My mother cried in that courtroom all those years later because the person that she loved the most kept back his most private pain from her – at a time when he was so innocent and vulnerable. There are people in your life who desperately want to be there for you. They want to give you their shoulders for support and tears, their ears to empathize and their hearts to help you heal.

Don't hide your quiet pain.

I share a phrase in my motivational speeches that I've coined to remind you of this: *In our imperfections, we make the deepest connections*. When you share your hurt, you give permission to others to help you heal.

And listen, I know that no one is immune to this fear of being vulnerable. When I became a police officer, I learned this firsthand at a tragic call.

VULNERABILITY IS NOT A VICE

When I was a police officer, I remember going to a call of a "sierra delta" – SD – police code for sudden death. The man worked in an auto factory and was found alone in an isolated area. After piecing together the story, I realized that he started choking, quickly slipped away, and – unable to clear the blockage on his own – died privately in seclusion.

My initial thought was, "Why would he run off when he clearly needed help to clear the blockage?"

Then I remembered something that a CPR instructor once told me. He said that dying alone after choking is more common than you think. Why? One word: Embarrassment.

Our instructor told us that many choking people first think, *Let me excuse myself so I don't disturb everyone else.* The default is to try to handle it on their own instead of asking for help. They are embarrassed about the situation and rather than asking for help, they quickly escape to avoid being vulnerable. Essentially the person would rather risk death than be vulnerable and ask for help.

How sad is that? A man lost his life for fear of embarrassment.

I remember judging that factory worker in my mind. I was angry at him. All death is unnecessary, but this one was completely avoidable. "All he had to do was ask for help," I thought with exasperation. But when I look back at his fear of vulnerability, I mentally conceded that I was no different.

I've cried alone more times than I can think of. More than I've ever cried in front of other people. When my dad died, I didn't cry at his funeral – and everyone thought I was weird. But since then, I've cried SO many times about him. I've soaked my pillow on many nights alone. About his death, about the discussions we never got to have, about the adult decisions that I was never able to discuss with him. He died when I was twenty, and even though he wasn't in my life the way other fathers were, I would have LOVED to discuss some "man" issues with him as an adult. Confession: tears are welling up in my eyes as I write this. He wasn't perfect, but I miss him.

If there's something you're going through, remember this: vulnerability is not a vice. You are not weak for feeling weak. You are not "less than" for needing help. You are not a burden when you reach out to those around you. Trust me – they will love you *more* for asking. They will appreciate you for trusting them with your pain. They may even open up and share similar feelings with you. Ask for help: not because you're weak, but because you want to remain strong. As I mentioned earlier, feelings are energy. They will find their way to the surface regardless of your attempts to suppress them. I learned this lesson in an embarrassing – yet humorous – way.

FEELINGS: THEY WILL COME OUT ANYWAYS

There are four words familiar to every husband: "Happy wife, happy life." Basically, when your wife is happy, everyone in the house is happy. When she's not, well.... The bottom line is this: I try to make sure my wife is happy as much as possible, and sometimes that means compromise. One of the small compromises that I make is watching movies with her that you might know as "chick flicks": dramas or romantic movies that tend to appeal more to female audiences.

Remember that "Kwesi cries alone" thing? Well, that came to an abrupt halt near the end of a movie we watched together.

I'm typically not affected by sad or romantic moments of movies – not to the point of tears, anyway. However, it was different during the movie *You're Not You,* starring Oscar winner Hilary Swank. Quick synopsis: Swank plays a classical pianist named Kate Parker. Parker is diagnosed with ALS (a debilitating motor neuron disease commonly known as Lou Gehrig's disease). She hires a caregiver and develops a close friendship with her. As the ALS slowly takes away Parker's ability to walk and move, she knows that death is coming. On her final night she demands to be left alone to die in her bed. At first her compassionate caregiver reluctantly agrees, but her love for Parker moves her to disobey the command. She rushes into the room, embraces Parker, and holds her as she takes her last breath. (I know, right? DEEP!)

So silly Kwesi watches this movie, and during this dramatic scene tries to hold back his tears. The wife is on the couch bawling her eyes out next to him, but Kwesi is like "Nope! No tears. I don't cry in front of people!"

Well, he fails in his attempt to be stoic – miserably. After Parker takes her last breath, there's a moment of silence, then Kwesi lets out what can only be described as loud, uncontrollable bawling. Tears flow uncontrollably, snot flows, he's a hot mess! What does the wife do? She laughs at him. Why? Because she could see he was trying so hard *not* to cry, that the crying was actually *more* intense because of the effort not to. "Now you know," she says. "Just let it out when you feel it."

Just let it out when you feel it.

Feelings are energy. Energy doesn't disappear. It goes somewhere. The feelings you hold in will come out anyways. Contained frustration can come out as misdirected anger. Contained jealousy as bullying or mean behavior. Contained sadness as self-medication or self-harm. It's all energy and it is vital that you express your feelings and get that energy out.

Let's talk about some ways to do that.

DISENTANGLE YOUR THOUGHTS

The studies vary, but on average, humans think about six thousand thoughts per day. That's hundreds of thoughts every hour. Is it any wonder that most people are sometimes overwhelmed? If you don't have an outlet for your thoughts and feelings, they *will* come out in some way. Remember, thoughts and feelings are energy.

In his book *A New Earth*, author Eckhart Tolle states that emotion is the body's reaction to your mind, so feelings flow from thoughts. Everything that you do comes from feelings and thoughts. That's how important it is to recognize what you think and feel. But that can be hard.

Regarding the six thousand thoughts, it's important to disentangle the jumble of thoughts in your mind so that you can have more peace and improve your relationship with yourself and others.

How do you do that? One way is by journaling.

Journaling is the process of applying left-brained analytical activity (writing), with right-brained freedom to wander. Amongst all those thoughts you have, your mind can pull out the ones worth pondering.

Journaling has been proven to help build self-confidence, reduce anxiety, and increase self-awareness. Make no mistake: journaling IS therapy, and it's one of the best ways to untangle your mind and bring clarity to your life.

I created a journal with prompts to get you started. You can find it here:

www.kwesimillington.com/store.

Although journaling can be an amazing technique on your mental health journey, reaching out to speak to someone when you are hurting can be, well, freeing.

OPEN UP

I read this quote in a magazine once and it really stuck with me: "I basically told my dad, 'Look, I've been thinking a lot about dying.' It was one of the most freeing moments of my life to get to share that with someone."

Many people who go through depression – especially boys and men – feel that they need permission to share those feelings. This may be heavy to read, but we need to discuss this. A study was conducted by the Centre for Addiction and Mental Health (CAMH), Canada's largest mental health teaching hospital and one of the world's leading research centers in its field (www.camh.ca). The study outlined the following statistics:

- Canada ranks 6th in suicide rates out of 33 countries examined in North, Central and South America.
- In Canada, there are, on average, almost 11 suicides *per day*.
- More than 75 percent of suicides involve men, but women *attempt* suicide 3 to 4 times more often.
- Young people aged 15 to 24 are more likely to experience mental illness and/or

substance abuse disorders than any other age group. (This is one of the main reasons that I speak to students!)

- Suicide is the second leading cause of death for people aged 15 to 24. In 2018, it was the *leading* cause of death for children aged 10 to 14. Yet…
- The average wait times for children and youth are 67 days for counseling and therapy and 92 days for intensive treatment.

Regardless of your gender and age, being honest and open with feelings of despair or depression *can* be truly freeing. But from personal experience, I know it can be difficult. As opposed to physical disease, which most people disclose to others willingly and openly, we often want to keep our mental issues a secret. It's almost as if we think people will not believe what cannot be seen. A malignancy is easy to prove; an MRI, ultrasound or x-ray scan shows people the truth of the problem. However, depression doesn't show up on a scan. In both cases, we feel something is not right, but without proof, we fear doubt and derision. This HURTS. I know because this happened to me.

Before I was diagnosed with depression and Post-Traumatic Stress Disorder (PTSD), I was sent to a doctor by my employer at the time. During the appointment I was met with doubting questions and sarcastic looks by the doctor "assessing" me. (I put the word assessing in quotes because I believe her mind was made up before a single question was asked.) Imagine: you can't sleep, you're taking prescription drugs to feel normal, and you just want some answers – only to be met with someone who has decided that nothing is wrong with you. I resisted the tears in her office, but they flowed freely down my face and neck once I got back in my car afterwards. I'd never felt more alone and humiliated.

Thank God I got a second opinion and finally some answers – and appropriate diagnoses of Major Depressive Disorder and PTSD. I want to give a shout-out to my AMAZING psychologist Deborah and the amazing staff at the Operational Stress

Injury Clinic in London, Ontario, for their care and non-judgment.

Even with that confirmation, however, I didn't want to tell anyone. I was embarrassed to admit that I had a mental disorder. In my book *RISE*, I share a time when I was sitting at the edge of my bed, where my face was soaked with tears, and my hand was full of pills, and I didn't want to be here anymore. I felt that admitting weakness made me weak, but the opposite is the truth. *Admitting weaknesses is the ultimate strength*. Once I got past abandoning and suppressing the truth and moved on to acknowledging the facts and allowing others in on my pain, I started to take the first steps toward recovery.

If you have ever felt anything close to what I've written about here – or worse – do this today: tell someone. Tell someone who loves you and supports you the truth. Tell them about your darkest moments. When you free your thoughts and feelings from the recesses of your mind, you free yourself from shouldering your burdens alone.

Open up.

YOUR FIVE F's

You might be reading this and thinking, Kwesi, I've never felt that low and I don't think I need therapy or anything, but sometimes I do feel down and would like to talk to someone.

I got you. Here's a way to simplify the often-difficult process of reaching out to others either for help, or simply to connect. Speaking to students has taught me an easier way to practice vulnerability. I call them the **five F's**.

1. Do you remember the **first** time you tried something and it didn't go according to plan?
2. How about a **failure** you've experienced and how it made you feel?
3. Do you have a personal **flaw** that embarrasses you or causes shame?
4. Or does something **frustrate** you that you rarely talk about?
5. What do you secretly **fear**?

These are your five F's: firsts, failures, flaws, frustrations, and fears.

The word "vulnerable" is defined in the Oxford Dictionary as "susceptible to physical or emotional attack or harm."

Many people fear that if they share personal details such as their five F's, their feelings or private pain, others will ostracize them or see them as "less than." I've learned that the exact opposite is true. When you are courageous enough to share your lowest moments, fears, and feelings with others, there's a two-way benefit that results. For you, the burden is lightened since someone else is helping you carry it.

For the other person, they feel more connected to you, less alone, and it gives them permission to be open and vulnerable as well.

How do I know this? Because I've spoken to thousands of students across North America and around the world as a professional speaker. I share my flaws, my fears, and my failures. And after every presentation I have at least a handful of students who always say to me, "Thank you for sharing your story. This is what I'm dealing with."

I've had students share that they've been bullied, experienced difficult personal situations, and even suicidal ideations. None of this open vulnerability would have happened had I not been open and vulnerable first. If you need someone to have a confidential conversation with (or if you are a parent who wants someone to talk to your preteen or teenager), reach out to me at kwesi@kwesimillington.com.

Our next chapter starts with a key lesson that I learned about mental health while in prison. But first, let's discuss how to create a stronger connection with those around you.

UNBREAKABLE BLUEPRINT:

REACH OUT

#1 – This one is just for you: Outline a quiet pain that you've experienced. Write out the details in your journal, including what happened, who was involved and the emotions that you felt. Now write down the names of one or two people that you trust and could have shared that with but didn't. Imagine what their response might have been and write that down. Would it have been supportive? Judgmental? How would they have responded? It's up to you if you want to share this with someone or keep it private.

#2 – Watch a "tear-jerker" movie. One of those movies that will likely make you sad. When you get to the heavy parts, notice if you are open to letting your emotions out or if you are a suppressor (like I was). When you watch other movies of any type, notice any emotions that make you uncomfortable. Chances are there's a story behind your resistance to show a certain feeling.

#3 – Make a list of some of your 5F's: Your firsts, failures, flaws, frustrations, and fears. Keep a running list and add to it as you remember more. Now… courage time! Share one or two of them with someone you trust. It can be the person you mentioned in #1 or someone else. Make a note in your journal about how they responded. Was it the response you expected or not? How did it feel to share? As time passes, note how you feel when you share future F's, and if the person you shared with starts to open up more to you (I think they will!).

PHRASES TO REMEMBER

The Bully Rule – Only broken people try to break other people.

The Connection Rule – In our imperfections, we make the deepest connections.

The Journaling Rule – The process of writing is the path to healing.

Chapter 5

Review Your Wins

You can't connect the dots looking forward; you can only connect them looking backwards.

– *Steve Jobs*

OCTOBER 31, 2017

I walk through the heavy metal door at the Maplehurst Correctional Complex to start my two-and-a-half-year sentence for perjury – a crime I never committed. The sun is shining, but I feel dark and empty inside. At least my wife is *outside*. The sun will dry my tears off her shoulder. I'm scared – terrified, actually. I'm not sure what the prison experience is like for a police officer. It's not the safest environment for *anyone*, but for a law enforcement professional who may have thrown some of these same guys in jail? Let's just say I didn't expect to be welcomed with high-fives!

Fortunately, the warden pulls me aside as I'm emptying my pockets and giving my personal belongings to a guard.

"We don't want to mix you in with the general population, for obvious reasons," he says with a knowing look. He knows that as a police officer walking into jail, I'm nervous, to say the least. "So," he continues, "we'll be placing you in solitary for the time being."

Solitary confinement is reserved as punishment for prisoners. Often commonly called "the hole," these cells are small isolation units where prisoners are placed away from the rest of the prison population. Confinement is termed "solitary confinement" once a prisoner has spent more than 22 hours in isolation. There is little to no meaningful contact with anyone, making the time in solitary very lonely – and mentally damaging.

Studies have shown that extensive time spent in solitary confinement leads to mental and psychological damage, including insanity and even suicide. In an attempt to curb the cruelty caused by extended isolation, the United Nations created what are commonly known as the "Mandela Rules" (named after the late South African president Nelson Mandela who spent 27 years in prison, including many years in solitary confinement). These rules included a recommendation that no one spend more than 15 days consecutively in solitary confinement. In 2019, Canada agreed and passed a bill with the same recommendation. My time in isolation did not abide by that advice.

I would eventually spend 30 days in isolation, the first seven in a prison at Maplehurst, and the duration at the Joyceville Correctional Facility in Kingston, Ontario. Believe it or not, my second solitary cell was an upgrade! First and most importantly, I went from a concrete "bed" to a metal one. Both probably sound equally uncomfortable, but I assure you that the difference between sleeping on a concrete slab, and a metal frame are night and day. Attempting to sleep on concrete with nothing but the equivalent of a gym mat and a thin blanket as padding was an impossible task. (Concrete does not yield to the natural curves of the human body). The pain all over my body was relentless, and I spent more time at night crying in my sheets than sleeping in them. So, when I tell you that the transfer to Joyceville and upgrade to a metal bed with an actual mattress was a godsend, I mean it.

That was my first "win" when I was in prison, but it wouldn't be my last. Something happened a few weeks into my sentence that might have been considered insignificant for some, but for me it was life-changing.

THE SMALLEST JOY

Can you remember something small that made you extremely happy? It may have been very insignificant in any other context, but in the moment, it provided you so much joy?

I'll get to my marvelous moment in just a minute, but first some trivia for you.

When I was led into my solitary cell, I was given a "kit," It included the following: a bar of soap, disposable razor, toothbrush and toothpaste, and a towel. (A student at a speech asked me this once so let's get this out of the way – there was already toilet paper in the cell. ☺) However, something was missing. Can you guess what it was?

Here's a hint... being a black man, I typically have drier skin – much drier – than other races. That hint probably gave the answer to you... it's moisturizer. Specifically – ChapStick. It may not seem like much, but after three weeks with zero products for hydrating my skin, I was in a lot of discomfort. In fact, my dry, cracked lips downright hurt. (Needless to say, when my wife was finally able to transfer some money into my "prison account," my first purchase was ChapStick.)

Picture the scene: I sit down, tear open the package, and apply desperately needed moisture to my lips. The relief sets in...and I start to cry. Not tears of sadness – but of joy. Then a few seconds later, I start to laugh. (Sounds crazy, right? One of my nicknames in school was "Crazy Kwesi," so I guess I finally lived up to the moniker!)

Here's why I laughed. I was thinking, This little thing has given me SO much joy – even in this prison cell!

Then an idea hits me. I wonder what other small joys I can think of, even in the midst of my incarceration. So, I take out paper and pen, and begin to write down everything I can think of to be grateful for. Warm blankets, clean clothes, free food (not great, but free).

This is the start of my list. Not much, but these are things that many people who are NOT incarcerated do not have.

As I wrote, my heart started to lift. I started to smile. And just for a minute, I completely forgot that I was sitting on a hard, metal prison bed. That feeling made me realize something very important that I now share with audiences when I speak: *When you celebrate what you have every day, every day becomes a celebration*. Was I popping champagne in prison? Of course not. But every time I wrote down what I was grateful for, my mood lifted – even if just for a moment.

I've never stopped the practice. Once I was released, I continued, and every morning to this day begins the same way – I pull out my journal and write down two or three things I'm grateful for. At the very least, I spend a few moments contemplating the blessings in my life.

Try doing this: Every day, don't be like most people who pick up their phones before they get out of bed. (Studies show 90 percent of people are on their phones within the first five minutes of waking.) Instead, write down what you are grateful for in your life. And don't just write it down – feel the gratitude. Say "I'm grateful for…" out loud.

There are crappy moments that happen throughout your day – this is unavoidable. But YOU have control over the first few moments of each day. Make them moments of small miracles…moments of gratitude. Make each morning a win. Then do your best to avoid what many fall into – the comparison trap.

THE COMPARISON TRAP

Nothing will steal your joy faster – and convince you more that you are flawed and imperfect – than comparing yourself to other people. I've both learned the truth of this and fallen victim to it more times than I care to count. From comparing the cheap bargain-store shoes I wore in middle school to those with Reebok Pumps and better, to comparing my business to more successful entrepreneurs as an adult, I've felt the pain of "less… than."

Less popular than…

Less successful than…

Less ripped than…

Less confident than…

Less…you name it, I've felt it. Have you?

Listen, comparison can be a good thing. You can compare yourself to someone at the gym, and that can motivate you to work harder on your own physique. You can compare yourself to someone successful in their job or business and be motivated to reach new levels of financial success yourself. You can even compare yourself in many areas that energize you to move forward in your own life. Unfortunately, however, comparison often leads to jealousy, depression, and gut-wrenching feelings of worthlessness. And let's be honest, social media is at the heart of the problem.

We don't need to discuss the benefits of social media. You are smart and aware enough to know that social media has its positives and advantages. You also know deep down that anytime you've had emotional lows or felt worse about who *you* are, one or both of two things were true: either (a) scrolling through the feed of your favorite social app *caused* the negative feelings, or (b) you *already* felt low, you went online for a distraction, and ended up feeling worse as a result.

Do yourself and your mental health a favor: limit your time online, especially when you are feeling inferior or inadequate. Once you've conquered this, remember this advice: Honor your feelings.

HONOR YOUR FEELINGS

Everywhere you turn, it seems like there is someone trying to tell you how to be happier. They talk about finding your joy, your passion, your "bliss." There is nothing wrong with this advice, but it fails to honor the fact that sometimes you just feel down. Straight up. What's worse is that many of these same "pleasure pushers" try to convince you to just get past the pain and get back to feeling good. That's why I love the author Debbie Ford's book *The Dark Side of the Light Chasers* (one of my faves). In it she says this: "What you can't be with, won't let you be." In the book, Ford passionately pleads with the reader to accept *all* sides of themselves – the flawed and the fabulous. I love that.

For years – and even now, at many times – I play mental tug of war with myself. On the one side is acceptance – understanding that the down times and feelings are normal, and to be accepted. On the other side – the devil on my shoulder, if you will – is the admonishing side: the side of me that says "Feel better! Do something to get out of your rut!"

We run away from our dark sides too often, thinking that if we leave that door in the house locked, we'll forget about it forever. The truth is – the door isn't going anywhere. You pass it every day, and if you never enter and explore, you can never be fully you. One day after that thought came to me, I penned the following message and posted it online (@KwesiSpeaks on Instagram):

NORMAL

Have you ever felt anxious?
Normal.

Ever felt insecure? Normal.

Depressed? Normal.

Your range of emotions may have
a mental health diagnosis.

It also may not. Sometimes the
feelings you have don't need

labeling.

The kaleidoscope of life. It will bring everything out in you.

The good and the bad. The highs and the lows. Heaven and hell.

Treatment is necessary, but sometimes it's the solution too quickly reached for. Sometimes the cure for loneliness isn't a pill, it's a hug and a conversation.

Sometimes the cure for anxiety is a break from technology.

Sometimes the cure for pain is presence. Burning the past and future up with fire and living fully absorbed in RIGHT NOW.

Sometimes the cure for emptiness is purpose. And sometimes that purpose is a simple act of giving or kindness.

Life is beautiful. And it is ugly. It has joy and disappointment. It contains the magnificent AND the mundane.

The good doesn't last forever. Neither does the bad.

Don't make a permanent decision based on a temporary circumstance.

Don't make a single moment the meaning of your life.

Remember this: Mental health AND mental hurt are a part of life.

Together we can #riseabove.

#becomingunbreakable

Disclaimer: If you are on any medication for mental health issues, I am NOT telling you to stop. I'm not a doctor.

Here's what I've found: many students (and some adults) that I speak to have fooled themselves into thinking that when life has pits, pain, and problems, they need to do something to get rid of them as soon as possible. They push the pain down or away and believe they are weak if they wallow in their feelings for too long. This is simply not true. While I do believe that some people carry their past and pain for too long, it is also true that many don't honor their feelings enough. It's important to remember – as the passage above states – that "mental health AND mental hurt are a part of life." Honor your feelings without always labelling them – and take steps to protect your mental state at the same time. One of those ways is to redefine what you call a "win."

KEEPING WINS IN PERSPECTIVE

The author Eckhart Tolle has said that there is a path to true enlightened living. He outlines that the path to true mental freedom and peace comes with something called the three "non's." While keeping track of your wins is a key to mental health, sometimes it's also important to take stock of your emotional connection to what you call a "win." These three steps will help you keep it all in perspective.

NON-ATTACHMENT

I don't remember where I read this, but the author suggested that you take the following steps when dealing with anything you desire: first, imagine what you want vividly; second, think of the worst-case scenario of your life if you didn't get what you desire; and finally, think of the ultimate picture of your life with your desire fulfilled. Then take that picture and imagine putting it in a helium balloon, and letting it go into the universe.

This is the idea behind non-attachment. Wanting something with a reasonable level of ambition, without becoming obsessed at the expense of your sense of inner peace. When you can desire without drama or desperation, you have achieved the state of non-attachment.

Step two of the non-attachment process is very revealing. Examine your feelings when you imagine the worst-case scenario of not getting that thing you so desire. Does the state of "wanting" make you feel uncomfortable? When you can think about your goal and honestly feel okay if you never achieve it – while at the same time working towards it – you will feel a sense of peace. That peace is the feeling of non-attachment.

NON-RESISTANCE

There's a story I read once about a Zen Master. The Master was trusted in his hometown, until one day a teenage girl accused him of getting her pregnant. The parents of the girl spread the word about the

Master, and angrily shouted at him for violating their trust in him. To this accusation, he simply replied, "Is that so?" Later, when the baby was born, the girl's parents thrust the baby onto the Master and told him that he had to raise the baby since he was the father. Once again, he said to the parents, "Is that so?" He took the baby and raised it as his own.

Years later, the girl confessed to her parents that she had lied – the Master was not the one who impregnated her, but a boyfriend that she had been keeping secret from them. Embarrassed and ashamed, the parents approached the Master, apologized profusely for their mistake, and asked to take the child back as they knew the Master was not the father. To this request, the Master once again replied, "Is that so?" as he returned the child to the girl's family. The moral of this story is that both in falsehood and truth, the Master responded in the same way, refusing to personalize any event, good or bad.

What a lesson to remember! When people get under your skin, what is your response? When you are unjustifiably attacked, are you quick to jump to the defensive? Do you seek to defend your bruised ego as soon as possible? I know there are still times that I do, but when I'm able to keep a calm demeanor when being attacked, it gives me a peaceful perspective on the situation.

Here's one way to practice non-resistance: when you find yourself tempted to react when someone verbally attacks you or insults you, take three deep, conscious breaths while they are speaking. Then *before* you respond, let there be a few seconds of silence in between you. What you'll find is that there is something calming between thoughts and words – that space is called peace – and it will allow you to respond with poise and power.

NON-JUDGMENT

English playwright William Shakespeare wrote, "Nothing is either good or bad, but thinking makes it so." Our first inclination is to quickly label the events in our lives with a positive or negative generic label. Far too often, we place labels prematurely when it really depends on your vantage point. A snowfall is bad to a bus driver having to get students to school, but good (if not great) to a child with a toboggan. Non-judgment is not meant to simplify your problems, but simply reminds you to practice thinking about things without automatically judging them as positive or negative. There are situations where it is harder to find the positive aspects.

So just do this: try treating everything that happens to you as "scale neutral." Reserve your opinion initially. Don't be naïve and look at everything with "rose-colored" glasses; just take a moment when something happens. Let your reactions to situations flow from that stillness. There may be a lesson to learn or there may not be. Simply allow yourself to focus on the power of each present moment, trusting your inner guidance to direct your path. By allowing non-judgment to win the day today, you may look back at a "bad" situation tomorrow with a better and brighter understanding.

Nothing is perfect in this life. However, when you can look at situations without attaching yourself to outcome (non-attachment), without resisting (non-resistance), and without initially labeling (non-judgment), you will find that you don't feel the need for perfection that holds many people back from being truly happy. Let's end this chapter with what I call the "Self-Esteem Sunset Activity."

THE SELF-ESTEEM SUNSET ACTIVITY

So, you've minimized your comparison to others on social media. You are starting your days by writing down and feeling what you are grateful for. You've even remembered to stay non-attached to wins.

Then you walk out the door, and someone – or something – disturbs your day and throws you off. Let's face it, no matter how "Zen" your day starts, you don't always end your day with the same peaceful and positive mindset that you created when your day began. That's why it's essential to "bookend your day" – start and finish each day with deliberate practices that build your mental health.

Have you ever had trouble falling asleep after something you watched online right before bed? Most people give no thought to what they consume before closing their eyes. Studies have shown that your subconscious mind is much more powerful than your conscious mind. And when is your subconscious mind most receptive? When you are sleeping. Imagine giving that powerful mind of yours thoughts of positivity and self-worth before going to sleep. How much better would your life be? How much happier and self-confident would you be? Much more. So, let's add a very simple activity before going to bed to help you improve your life. I call it the "self-esteem sunset activity."

It's a complicated title, but a simple one-minute activity. Keep a journal by your bed and right before you go to sleep, write down one, two or three wins that you had for that day. Now don't overthink this: it's not about major academic or life wins – but of course write those down if you had them!

When I give this exercise to students (and adults), they often get stuck because they have messed up the definition of a "win" and have made it too restrictive. Most people think a win has to be something grand – something that they would be congratulated or compensated for if others knew about it. Realistically, these major wins are not everyday occurrences, so when this is all that you look at as a win, it makes it hard to think of something to write down daily.

Let's expand your definition of a win. Did you complete your homework? That's a win. Did you make a delicious breakfast or dinner for yourself? Win. Did you give a compliment to or do something nice for someone today? Another win.

Let's reduce the magnitude of what we call a win. Write down something daily. Two things will happen when you do: first, your powerful subconscious mind takes in the message that you are a success. Isn't that a better thought to put into your mind instead of that last episode of your favorite show? The second positive side effect of writing down your wins is that it helps you to realize that no matter what is going on in your life, there are at least a few things going well for you.

Imagine your life when you write down your daily wins. Actually, let's shrink that – imagine your week. Let's face it, there are times when you don't have the best week. You may have moments when you think, *Why did I even get out of bed today (or this week)?* When you have those thoughts (and we all do), review your wins for the week. Remember them. Re-live the moment in your imagination.

Here's what will happen: you'll realize that life isn't about big moments, it's about small daily victories. Start tonight with your win from today, and I'll see you in the next chapter where we will talk about how to feel great about yourself every day.

UNBREAKABLE BLUEPRINT:

REVIEW

#1 – Use the screen time checker on your phone (or time yourself in some other way). Do this for a week and track the average time that you spend online during the day. Take that number and reduce it by at least 10 percent. For example, if you spend an average 3 hours online daily, aim to reduce your time by 18 minutes. (3 hours =180 minutes x 10 percent) Think of something creative and "unplugged" that you can do for 18 minutes a day. And don't you dare say you don't have the time! You are spending it online, so it's ALREADY being used. Just redirect the usage. After you implement your new activity, write down your thoughts and feelings about your lifestyle change. Do you feel more refreshed? Better or worse? Remember self-awareness is the key to confidence and thriving through change.

#2 – Write down feelings that you have that you consider negative. Do you feel anxious at times? Fearful? Jealous? After you write the feelings down, write this phrase: "I am normal for feeling…." Then fill in the words you wrote down. Say the sentence out loud to remind yourself that we all have negative feelings at times, and you are normal for feeling.

#3 – Write down your daily wins before bed each night. One win is all that's necessary but write more if you can think of them. Then do this – at the end of each week review your daily wins from each night. The more you do this, the better you'll feel, regardless of what's going on in your life.

PHRASES TO REMEMBER

The Chapstick Rule – When you celebrate what you have every day, every day becomes a celebration.

The Self-Acceptance Rule – What you can't be with, won't let you be.

The Self-Esteem Sunset Rule – Life isn't measured by big moments; it's measured by small victories.

Chapter 6

Recognize Your Value

There's a crack in everything. That's how the light gets in."

– *Leonard Cohen*

THE EDGE OF THE BED

Warning: This section will get heavy. If you feel triggered, please reach out to someone you can talk to professionally. And of course, if you just want to talk, I'm here as well:

kwesi@kwesimillington.com

The following is an excerpt from my first book, RISE: The 8 Keys to Overcoming Adversity & Living a Life You'll Love.

I can remember contemplating suicide.

I can remember thinking the question. I had the powerful pain killers. I had the equally effective sleeping pills. I sat on the edge of my bed, asking myself one question: "How many of these do I need to take? How many – so I just don't have to wake up anymore."

The year was 2011. I had just been charged a few months before with perjury. For the first time in my policing career, I really felt that it was over. I didn't know what to do with my life. Just a job? No. For years it was how I identified myself. How I saw myself. Who I was. If I could no longer be a police officer, what else would I do?

The real question was: "Who am I REALLY?"

Marianne Williamson, author of the book "Return to Love," states that "taking responsibility for our lives means taking responsibility for our thoughts." My thoughts were swirling in negative. The average person thinks thousands of thoughts per day, and many of those are repeated thoughts. All that I could think at the edge of the bed was that I had no worth. At that moment, no job, no career, meant no personal worth. And since I had no personal worth, I believed that I had no reason to live."

I remember that moment at the edge of the bed clearly. I thought that being a police officer was all that gave me any worth. I could not have been more wrong. What you do is not who you are. What you cannot do does not determine who you are, either.

Since writing that, I've had moments when I've felt hopeless, moments when I just started crying for no apparent reason other than just to give my overflowing sadness an outlet. And moments when I've never felt more alone.

Conversely, since writing that, I've also had moments of pure joy, moments of happiness, moments of connection. Throughout it all, I've realized that the low moments stemmed from one thought: "I'm a complete failure." But the truth is, I was not a failure. What I've come to realize is this: just because you've been redirected, doesn't mean that your path to success has been refused or blocked. Just like driving to your destination, there are many ways to get there. Besides, there IS value in failure.

THE VALUE OF FAILURE

Do this one thing: stop looking at your failures as embarrassment. You know the ones...that thing you tried and looked foolish doing. The time you spoke up and wish you didn't. The risk you took that backfired.

Stop looking back at your failures with shame and regret. Most people don't have your courage. They stay safe, free of judgment, free of ridicule...and free of passion or purpose. They never try – and then they die.

That's NOT you. At least you tried something. Was it a risk? Probably. A failure? Yes. Embarrassing? Definitely. But it was also informative – you learned your limits and what or who to stay away from. You played in the danger zone of uncertainty that most people never dare to tread. You *trusted* yourself – you believed in yourself. You trusted that you could take on a new challenge and win. And you were right – you *are* right. You didn't fail. You just needed more time. Maybe more practice. Maybe a course, a coach, or a mentor. And in acting – you showed the world that nothing is impossible. Sometimes we just need more time or knowledge to achieve it.

So do this one thing: stop looking at your failures as embarrassment. Go ahead and fail. Be happy, not ashamed, when you look at past failures. It means you tried. It means you trusted yourself. It means you're willing to fully live. Now let's talk about another way to help you put failure behind you. I call it "The Hesitant Yes."

THE DRIVING TEST

Do you have a driver's license? Whether you do or not, you'll relate to this story. When I got my license, it was like freedom for me. I didn't have to ask anyone for a ride, I had my own. My first car was a black Nissan Sentra, my next one was an Acura of similar size. I always drove smaller vehicles and was comfortable in them. However, when I got to police training, they handed me the keys to a much bigger vehicle: a Ford Crown Victoria. Maybe for some that wouldn't be a big deal, but when you have to navigate through an obstacle course at a high rate of speed, while also trying not to hit numerous orange pylons positioned in strategically difficult places on 90-degree turns, that bigger car may as well have been a bus. Welcome to my final driving test at police college!

The task was simple enough: drive a clean run through the obstacle course in the time given, or be kicked out of training, leave Regina, fly home to Toronto with my tail between my legs, and look for another job. No pressure! With sweat soaking my training uniform and an instructor sitting beside me, I pulled the Crown Victoria to the start line. Three…two…one…Go!

Straightaways – easy. Wide turns – easy. I am motoring through the track with relative ease, until I get to the three 90-degree turns and those dreaded orange pylons. Set up deliberately to provide a supreme challenge to recruits, this is the hardest portion of the course. And true to "I can't drive this massive car" form, I knock them all down. First run: fail.

I drive slowly to the start line once again. Three…two…one…Go! I cautiously press the gas pedal, pushing the car to the breakneck speed of… 40 kilometers per hour!

The instructor – who kind of looks like a shorter Tony Robbins – reminds me of my mistake. "Kwesi, you remember you have to beat the clock too, right?"

I don't. Foot to the floor, I pick up speed, and by the time I get to the 90-degree turns, I'm back on pace to make it in the allotted time. I slow right down…any slower and I would have been parked! I make it through one turn, two, three. I'm through! I look excitedly at my instructor.

He doesn't return my look of joy. "You hit the pylons, Kwesi." He sounds as disappointed as I was about to be. He was rooting for me to pass. You see, he didn't only *look* like Tony Robbins, he was as positive and typically motivating as Robbins was too! Always the first to provide a kind and supportive word during training.

I feel badly not only for myself, but for disappointing him! At the finish line, I am spent. Ready to pack up my bags – and pack in my dreams of becoming a police officer – and return to Toronto.

Sometimes you have to say yes. Sometimes you have to speak about *future* success, even if you feel like a *present* failure. Sometimes you have to be willing to believe in yourself, even when there is no indication that you will succeed.

That "hesitant yes" is how Shonda Rhimes, the American television producer who created the hit shows *How to Get Away with Murder* and *Grey's Anatomy*, became a massive success. A previously shy and hesitant introvert, Rhimes decided to spend a year saying YES to everything that scared her. The result became a New York Times Best-seller entitled *Year of Yes: How to Dance It Out, Stand in the Sun and Be Your Own Person*. In the book she said that we need to say YES to everything scary. YES to everything that takes you out of your comfort zone. YES to everything that feels like it might be crazy. That's what is called the "hesitant yes." Rhimes wrote the book after I was in police college but, rewind the clock, and that's the exact type of "yes" I was asked to give.

"Last run, Kwesi. I know you feel down. I know you're nervous."

Obviously...my armpits are drenched! My instructor (I'll call him Mini Robbins because I don't remember his real name) asks me a question I'll never forget: "Kwesi, can you give me ONE clean run?" It sounds so simple. One clean run...the difference between success and failure, winning and losing, walking alongside my troop on graduation day... or returning home to begin a new job search. One word changes my life... I look at Mini Robbins and simply say, "YES. I can."

I would love to describe that last run to you in detail, but honestly it's such a blur that I'm not even sure if I was actually driving or floating! Sure there was the "Three...two...one...Go!" I'm pretty sure I pushed the pedal and was the one sitting behind the wheel. And I'm fairly confident that Mini Robbins was shaking MY hand and shouting at me with exuberance: "YOU DID IT! YOU PASSED!" But honestly, I don't remember. What I DO recall is marching with my troopmates on May 16, 2005, and receiving the badge that made me an official member of the Royal Canadian Mounted Police.

What "hesitant yes" do you need to say in your life? At some point, you have to believe in your value. You have to believe that no matter if you –

or anyone in your life – has told you "no," you have a choice. You do NOT have to believe them (or the negative voice in your head). If there is something you want to do, be or have, say yes to yourself. It's okay if you're afraid. It's okay if you're unsure. It's okay if you're hesitant. But say yes anyways. Even if you've heard "no" a million times, all you ever need is ONE yes. And that yes comes from you.

THE OTHER SIDE OF THE COIN

As I got better at it, police driving went from something I hated to something I loved. But here's something I want you to remember: You don't have to love something just because you have to do it. You don't have to get excited about something just because everyone else does. There are far too many people who have let other people decide what they value or consider success. There are times when being satisfied is better than trying to be a soaring success. There are occasions when simply accepting who you are and your current situation is more empowering than trying to climb to the top of the mountain.

I learned the power of this acceptance when I picked up a gun for the first time at police college. Unlike many other recruits, police college represented the first time that I ever held a gun in my life. This may sound strange, but holding a gun intimidated me. Feeling the weight of it. Loading it with bullets. But most of all, firing it for the first time. A 9mm gun doesn't have much kick compared to most guns that one can shoot, but for someone who had never held one before it was downright shocking – and overwhelming. I thought, *There's NO way I'm going to get better at shooting this thing!*

The first time at target practice confirmed my fears. We shot about 25 meters from the target, and I was nowhere close to the center. *I'm in trouble*, I thought. To successfully complete training, a score of 200 out of a possible 250 was required. When I first started shooting, scores of 100 were the norm for me.

No need for suspense here – eventually I would obtain the 200 score on test day, without the "last chance" scenario that I faced with police driving. The only reason that was possible is due to the literally HUNDREDS of hours (and thousands of rounds of ammunition) that I spent at the range to become a proficient shooter. I'm proud to say that after becoming a police officer, I even obtained the "cross pistols" certification when I tested again on my required periodic retraining test. ("Cross pistols" is awarded when you achieve a score of 225 or higher out of 250.)

However, I never gained the comfort level that other officers have with guns. In training we had to shoot 9mm handguns, shotguns, and a rifle – and I disliked all of them. Conversely, many of the other officers I met in training and in the field loved guns. They went to ranges during their spare time and chose to shoot all types of guns (MUCH more powerful) for recreation. A part of me always thought I was strange for never having that mentality. I thought I was supposed to like guns and action and risky behavior as a police officer, but that just wasn't me.

While many of my male counterparts were into the high-action, high-adrenaline calls, I was the one who liked the family calls, slow-paced cases, and visiting schools (which is probably why moving into Youth Motivational Speaking was a natural fit for me). When I worked in Richmond, British Columbia, there was actually a Youth Section – a "rotation" where your days as an officer were dedicated exclusively to working with young people and in schools. I put in my name to work in that section before the whole Vancouver airport / perjury situation occurred – and was derided for it. Other officers made fun of me, claiming that I didn't want to do "real" police work, a.k.a. drug enforcement, murder investigations, etc. And I let their mocking get to me. I quietly planned to apply for the Youth Division, wondering if that – coupled with my lack of enthusiasm for guns – made me less of a police officer...and less of a man.

I know now that this is "herd mentality" – the tendency of people to be affected and influenced by the majority. It's why when one person bullies, others join in. It's why sports fans get so rowdy – and sometimes destructive. And it's why many "manly" officers thought that working in a section devoted to young people was weak.

There's an experiment that proved the power of the majority group. It was famously termed the Asch Conformity Experiments (or Asch paradigm). In 1951, psychologist Solomon Asch brought together groups of eight male college students and gave them a simple task. Each student viewed a card with a straight line on it, followed by another card with three lines labeled A, B and C. One of the lines was the same length as that on the first card, with the other two lines being clearly longer or shorter. Each participant was asked to say aloud which line on the second card matched the length of the line on the first card.

Here's the catch: out of the eight students, seven were actors and were told to unanimously give an incorrect response. The one unsuspecting student was clearly bewildered by the incorrect responses, yet they doubted their own belief in the correct answer. The results were not overwhelming, but still telling. In 36.8 percent of the trials, the innocent student conformed to the majority – even though the answer was clearly incorrect. Asch reported that this was surprising, since the answer was so obvious that 100 percent of the innocent students should have answered correctly. (I encourage you to look up "Asch Conformity Experiment" on YouTube).

The experiment proves that, in the midst of an opposing majority, the pressure is strong to doubt your own thoughts, feelings, and values. When you can stand your ground regardless of what others pressure you to think, say or do, you will feel a sense of self-worth and confidence.

So be who you are, love what you love, and stand strong in what you value. As for me, I love working with young people…and I'm still not a fan of guns.

RELAX

There's a quote from the spiritual text *A Course in Miracles* that would be empowering for you to remember: "Nothing you do or think or wish or make is necessary to establish your worth." This quote constantly reminds me to stop obsessing over what I may or may not accomplish.

I used to measure my value by what I was able to put out in the world. This is normal – we are trained to be like this. From the moment you were born, you were validated based on your actions. Parents express joy when babies smile and accomplish various milestones. Grades are assigned on schoolwork. Raises are awarded based on job performance. Productivity can be positive, but measuring your intrinsic value by what you put out into the world is a recipe for disappointment.

Compliments, adoration, or a higher grade or paycheck; welcome them, work for them, but don't crave them at the expense of your self-esteem. When striving for excellence becomes striving for acceptance and admiration, you lose the fact that you are ALREADY a miracle.

FLOAT, DON'T STRUGGLE

I started to swim at a young age. In fact, I marched through the swim-course levels on my way to becoming a certified Lifeguard. I remember building the endurance needed to stay afloat without touching the edge of the pool. One day our instructor mentioned something interesting. She said that the more frantic the non-swimmer gets trying to stay afloat, the faster they will sink. She taught us that staying calm, relaxing into smooth strokes while swimming made it easier to both stay afloat and quickly move through the water.

How many times have your feelings of frustration resulted exclusively from struggling instead of floating along through the waters of life? How often have you gotten irritated and annoyed because you couldn't be, do or have something? Is it possible that the goal you missed was one you weren't even supposed to be aiming for? I know there have been times when I spend far too much energy fighting unhappily for what I eventually ended up not even needing or wanting. The older I get, the more I realize that the unfolding of my own experiences is simply life's way of teaching the lessons that are meant exclusively for me.

Adopt a "float, don't struggle" mindset in your life. Settle into your experiences, instead of fighting the current of life. When you relax into everything that you do, without exerting yourself trying to prove your value or worth to other people, you move through life with more confidence and self-esteem. Trying to impress will only depress you.

Let's finish this chapter with some exercises to help you remember that you are valuable and enough, just the way you are.

UNBREAKABLE BLUEPRINT:

RECOGNIZE

#1 – Think about a past failure you've had. Detail the situation on paper: what happened, who was involved, and how it made you feel. Then do this: write down at least ONE way in which that failure made you stronger. Outline what you learned, and how you can use that failure to grow as a person. This will help you recognize that failures are simply learning opportunities and paths to becoming the person you're meant to be.

#2 – Now think about a success that you had to work for – maybe even one you failed at originally. This doesn't need to be big. A student at one of my motivational speeches once said that she finally baked a delicious cake after ruining the recipe numerous times! Remembering the times when you overcame failure to achieve success will help you to recognize your value.

#3 – Do you have a "hesitant yes" in your life? Maybe it's something from the past – a time when you said yes even though you doubted yourself (or others doubted you). Perhaps it's something that you want to say yes to but are afraid that you might be ridiculed for. Is there a yes you've said that made you more confident, or a yes you *should* be saying that will help increase your sense of self-worth?

PHRASES TO REMEMBER

The Universe Rule – Don't confuse refusal with redirection.

The Rooted-Tree Rule – Stand for something, or you'll fall for anything.

The "Where's Waldo?" Rule – Trying to impress, will only depress you.

PART III -- HOW YOU ACT

Chapter 7

Raise Others

Everything we do is either love or a call for love.

– Helen Schucman

BORROWED LIGHT

Do you know how moonlight is created? I probably learned it in school and then forgot the answer, so when I read it again a couple of years ago it really struck me as an important lesson for this chapter. The moon itself is dark. It doesn't produce any light. The reason you see that beautiful light on a clear, dark night is because the moon reflects the pre-existing light from the sun. Sunlight "bounces" off the moon and is redirected to us as what we call moonlight.

In essence, the moon "borrows" its light from the sun.

The same is true in life. There are times when we need other people. We are hard-wired for connection. Sometimes that means reaching out to others for help. And sometimes, as we'll discuss later, that means offering help to other people. No one gets through life without needing someone. No one is "self-made" as much as the term is tempting for the ego to take ownership of. There are two essential truths to realize to live a happier and more fulfilled life. Number one: we need each other; Number two: we need to help each other. These realizations came to me at one of the lowest moments of my life.

GETTING OUT OF THE BED

At the beginning of the last chapter, I talked about sitting at the edge of my bed, not wanting to be here anymore. Now, let me tell you what got me out of bed. I don't know what you believe, but I think that something spiritual happened in one of my lowest moments. Some call it a hunch – I think it was the voice of a Universal Power – I call it God. I didn't hear the words. I *felt* them. The thought that helped me get out of that bed was simple:

"Who needs me?"

I thought about my mother and the rest of my family. I thought about the friends who might miss me. Nowadays the answer is my wife and son. I realized then that your life's worth is not who you are, but who you are *to other people*. The more that you do for others, the more worthy you will feel of the life you have been given. That understanding changed my life. The simple question that followed was, "How can I do more for others?"

That same voice rushed into my mind and responded: "Find a gym."

One of my first coaching certifications was as a Personal Trainer and Lifestyle Wellness Coach. As I sat on that bed contemplating life outside of a policing career, that was all I had to fall back on. I thought, "*Even if I can't help someone as a police officer, I CAN help someone to live a healthier and more energetic life*. So I found a fitness center in my neighborhood, and they graciously gave me exactly what I needed: one client – one person to help.

According to the career website Workopolis, Canadians can expect to hold roughly 15 jobs in their careers. In the USA, the Bureau of Labor Statistics cited that individuals between the ages of 18 and 38 will hold more than 10 jobs. Regardless of where you are located, the message is simple: life is about change. Sometimes we create it; sometimes it is handed to you in the form of adversity. What I've found to be true is: the best way out of your funk, your down moments, your depressed and low times…is to get up and help someone.

YOU WERE BORN TO CARE

I once read a study about babies that was very telling. Within two weeks of being born, an infant will stop crying if they hear a recording of their own cries but will cry more loudly if they hear *another* baby crying or in distress. This proves that you were BORN to care about other people. If you choose not to help others, you are going against what you were born to do. It's in your nature to care.

However, our society has fooled you into thinking that it's cooler to not care, to be indifferent, to pretend that you don't have feelings for others. People have confused not caring what other people think of you, with not caring *about* other people. Many people make fun of, point out, and bully others as if their actions don't matter. They talk about "zero f***s given" and doing whatever you want without any thought of repercussions or consequences. And since most of this is done from behind a screen, the lack of face-to-face contact when such comments are made means we don't need to have any empathy. Screens and technology are making us behave more coldly toward each other. They shut down the parts of the brain that make you think, *Should I really say that?* Is it any wonder that the late Steve Jobs once said in an interview, when asked about his kids and the iPad: "They haven't used it. We limit how much technology our kids use at home."

Wait... didn't Steve Jobs' company *create* the iPad?

The obvious question is: Why would Jobs not want his kids to use something that his own company created? I don't know what his answer is. I do know that studies have proven that screen time reduces empathy. And why is empathy important? Quite simply, because without it we would all be psychopaths. I'm not kidding. Approximately 98 percent of people can empathize with others, and the other 2 percent are either psychopaths or narcissists. If you would prefer to stay away from one of those labels, but also feel the need or just want to keep up your screen time, it's vital to practice empathy.

So, what IS empathy? First off, it is NOT sympathy. Sympathy is feeling sorry for someone. It is looking at someone's pain or problems and saying, "That sucks!" You can have sympathy and just walk away. Empathy requires a bit more from you.

Empathy requires you to say, "I feel your pain." Sympathy *sees*. Empathy *feels*. And when you relate to and feel what someone else is going through, you are much more likely to want to help them. You feel connected to them. You are not only curious about what they are experiencing, but you validate them by listening to and imagining what they are feeling. Empathy improves relationships, reduces stress, and builds resilience. You were born empathetic, so just keep doing what you were born to do – care. I learned the power of this when I was in prison – from a teacher.

A NEW PERSPECTIVE

Have you ever judged someone without getting to know them? That's kind of a rhetorical question – we ALL have. Sometimes the pre-judgment even appears justified. This was the case when I was transferred from solitary confinement to minimum security. I started my unjustified prison sentence in solitary since it was decided that the inmates in the jail's general population wouldn't like to have a police officer in their midst. After all, as far as they're concerned, I may have put some of their friends in prison myself!

Eventually, my time in isolation ended and I found myself living in the minimum-security section of the prison in Kingston, Ontario. To give you perspective, this area housed everyone from those convicted of minor offenses, to registered sex offenders, all the way to those convicted of murder. (And yes, I met some of ALL three types!)

However, this section was a desired area since many of the offenders housed here were nearing the end of their sentences, and more privileges were afforded such as the ability to walk outside, access to a decent gym, and even work duties outside of the prison. Even the ones who still had longer times to serve (some "lifers" were even placed here after years of good behavior) knew that this was the safest place to be, because everyone had something to lose if they acted up. No one wanted to be placed in a more dangerous unit with tighter restrictions, so the mood was fairly calm and congenial – for a prison. When I met some of the other offenders I was reserved, of course, but eventually felt comfortable in the unit. However, that didn't stop me from judging.

I looked at everyone with my nose turned up. I thought, *Well, they deserve to be here. I don't! They are real criminals, and I'm better than they are!* Have you ever looked for the slightest of differences between you and someone else to justify a feeling of superiority?

Our society does it all the time. Shows like *Jerry Springer* and *Maury* (featuring Maury Povich) used to cater to the desire to feel superior to others. Even in my case when my reasons appeared logical, judging only served to build a wall between myself and the other prisoners. At first, I was okay with that – after all I wanted to remain anonymous – but since I was going to be around these men for a good amount of time, I began to realize that isolation and finger pointing were not going to be good daily habits to maintain. Fortunately, the need for a prison "job" brought me to James' office.

James is 6’6” tall. He towers over me as I walk into his office. He is well-dressed, and a master’s degree certificate hangs on his office wall. I’m instantly impressed and sit down across from him. He asks me if I’ve found a job at the prison yet. I say no. He mentions that he needs an English tutor to help the other inmates write their assignments with proper grammar and that he’d like me to take on the role.

I say yes – but mostly because the other job left for me was scrubbing toilets! He expresses that he's pleased that I’m taking the position, because the guys really need the help to get their high school diplomas.

Honestly, I’m not sure why he cares so much – so I ask him.

“James, I see your degree on the wall. I can tell you’re educated. Couldn’t you get a better, much higher paying job outside of the prison?” His eyebrows rise in acknowledgment. We both know he could make more money elsewhere. I continue, “So WHY are you here?”

His reply was simple: "Kwesi, 89 percent."

I look puzzled.

"Eighty-nine percent of prison inmates in Canada," he continues, "don't have a high school diploma. If I can help some of these guys get a diploma, get out there and get a good job, they won't be back here. I know there are many great teachers out there doing great work. I just know that I can make a big difference in here, so I chose this."

According to Correctional Service of Canada, the number of inmates who do not have a high school diploma nationwide is closer to 65 percent, however the impression on me was already made, regardless of the outdated percentage. I thought, *Wow, James is not even a prisoner, and he refuses to judge these guys, so why should I?*

He gave me a new perspective.

In the Bible, the book of Matthew contains one of the most well-known phrases in the world: "Do not judge, or you too will be judged." Most people regardless of their religious preferences know this timeless advice, but how often do we practice it? I've caught myself so many times breaking the rule, and James was just another reminder that I needed to look at the other inmates neutrally instead of judgmentally.

Think about the people in your life, as well as those you see online. Are you pre-judging people without knowing anything about them? Can you try to be less judgmental with the people in your life? Once I started tutoring, I learned more about the inmates. I learned their stories. I started to look at them not as "bad" people necessarily, but as good people – who just made some mistakes. Moreover, I realized that helping them gave me an added benefit: it helped me as well.

PAY IT FORWARD

In 2000, a movie was released called *Pay it Forward*. The young star, played by Haley Joel Osment (he was also the child star in *The Sixth Sense*), was challenged by a teacher in the movie to come up with a plan to change the world for the better.

The boy comes up with a project that he called "Pay it Forward." Essentially, whenever someone had a nice deed or favor done for them, they were not to pay it back – as in "do something nice for the giver" – but instead they were to do a favor for three other people instead.

For each of the three people receiving the sequential favor, they were assigned to do the same thing – do favors for three people of *their* choosing. The goal, of course, is to spread more kindness and love into the world.

Personally, I liked the movie, but was surprised to read that some critics called the movie "emotionally manipulative" as well as simplistically "blackmailing" people to be nicer. That was in the year 2000. See if you can find the movie – and let me know what you think (email me at kwesi@kwesimillington.com).

We live in a "Me first" world. People are so stressed out about their *own* problems, that they can't be bothered caring about the lives of others. Some see kindness as weakness, and frankly many people have simply painted the world with brushes from their past. Simply meaning they have pain that they are dealing with that they believe prevents them from even needing to care about others.

Here's what I know for sure – if you wait for your pain or problems to subside before reaching out to help others, you'll be waiting for the rest of your life. Tutoring in that prison taught me that no matter what you are going through, paying it forward – doing kind or helpful things for others – adds value to YOU. In my motivational speeches I remind students of this simple rule: *When you add value to others, YOU feel valuable*.

Listen, sometimes life sucks – I get it. Far too many people expect every day to be phenomenal. They expect excitement and happiness every day, but life doesn't work like that. There are ups and downs, highs and lows, moments of joy and moments of depression. However, there is one constant that always seems to work – when I find a way to add value to someone else, the days seem brighter, the burdens less heavy, and life feels more meaningful. And for me personally, my life as a motivational and professional speaker is all about paying forward the value that a teacher added to me when I was in high school.

THE TWO TEACHERS

Can you remember the most uplifting thing someone has ever said to you? Was it a teacher? Your parents? A friend? For me it was a high school English teacher – Mrs. S. She said something to me that not only gave me confidence, but it changed my life. Unfortunately, the main reason her compliment meant so much is because of a lingering insult that *another* teacher said to me a few years earlier.

Let's go back to Grade 6 art class. My teacher – we'll just call him Mr. C – was returning a painting assignment to the class. I don't remember what I was supposed to be painting, but I DO remember what Mr. C said to me before handing it to me. At the time I was a back-of-the-class student, one who doesn't put his hand up, and simply hopes to remain invisible for the duration of the school day due to a lack of confidence. (Know anyone like this?)

When Mr. C called me to the front to get my painting, I'll always remember what he said. With just the two of us standing at the front of a full class of students, he held my painting up, carefully turned left and right to ensure everyone could see it, then said these words:

"Hey everyone. Look at this painting Kwesi did. Doesn't it look like I used it to wipe my ass?"

A hush filled the room. A moment of silence. Then a few giggles and even some laughs from many of the students. Mr. C looked at me sarcastically, gave me the painting, and said, "Why did you even bother?"

Has someone ever hurt or made fun of you? Have you ever done what I call the "cover-up" response? Laugh it off or pretend in some other way that the insult didn't affect you? In that moment, I was in such a mix of shock, hurt and surprise, that I just laughed as I took the painting from Mr. C and sat down. I looked at a few of the other laughing students and chuckled along with them.

If you were sitting next to me in that class, you would have seen a smile on my face. It was forced – of course – as I tried to forget the most humiliating moment of my life. That is, until the end of class. As soon as I heard that bell, I ran to the bathroom as if I had to let out a pee that I'd been holding all day.

However, what I was holding in came out as I sat in that stall in the empty bathroom. Tears. A lot of tears. Years of tears, pain, and feelings of complete and utter inferiority flowed from my eyes in that stall. Memories of my spelling bee mishap and all my other failures rushed back into my mind. I just wanted to die in that moment. Literally. I thought, *What am I even doing on this planet? Why am I here?*

If you have ever felt alone, lost, unappreciated, hopeless, defeated, or worse, please reach out to me (kwesi@kwesimillington.com) because I understand you. I get that sometimes all you want is someone to say "You matter. You have worth. You are here for a reason." I truly believe you are. Unfortunately, people love to put others down (remember the *Jerry Springer* effect from earlier in the chapter?). It's rare that we run into people who take the time to raise others up. This is what I try to do as an inspirational speaker – remind you that you have value even if you can't see it yet. In Grade 6, I needed words of hope desperately. It took a few years, but in Grade 10, I finally got them – from an English teacher.

Mrs. S taught that English class, and I must say that I enjoyed it much more than Grade 6 art class, not just because of the teacher, but because frankly I was much better at English than art. Mrs. S confirmed that on one magical day (for me) when she was returning a marked essay to students in the class. She said my name, and I walked to the front of the room. By this time on my schooling journey, I hated walking to the front of the classroom – even just to receive a marked assignment. I stuck my hand out timidly.

Mrs. S confidently thrust my essay into the outstretched palm. Then she stopped, and my heart started to race. "What mistake did I make on *this* one?" I wondered. I looked into her eyes and saw something markedly different from what I saw in Mr. C's: kindness. Then she said the words that lifted both my head and my heart: "Kwesi, you're a gifted writer. Don't ever stop."

There are moments in your life where you can draw an imaginary line. There's "before" it happened, and "after." When Mrs. S gave me that compliment, that was one of those moments.

I'm not saying that life has been all roses and grand accomplishments since then, but she gave me something that I never had in school until that day: hope. Hope that I could *actually* do something well. Hope that I wasn't a complete failure in life. Hope that I could succeed. From that day forward, I never stopped writing. I've written journal entries that have become blogs and posts that have helped other people. I've written hundreds of poems, some of which were published in national publications. I've written three books *in addition* to the one you are reading now. And the words that I've written as speeches have inspired thousands of students, educators, and others around the world. I truly believe that much of that would never have been possible had Mrs. S not uttered that compliment to me all those years ago.

Mrs. S is one of my heroes. I have never been able to find and thank her, but perhaps you have the chance to thank your hero. Is there someone in your life who has uplifted you? Let them know that their words or actions have helped you. Let them know that they've raised you up. Selfishly, your gratitude to a hero is my way of saying thanks to mine.

And oh yeah, remember that sarcastic Mr. C from Grade 6 art class? One of my other heroes – my mom – marched into that school as soon as I told her what he said… and he was promptly fired.

UNBREAKABLE BLUEPRINT:

RAISE

#1 – Empathy is defined as "the ability to understand and share the feelings of another." This is not to be confused with sympathy. Imagine someone falls into a deep ditch. Sympathy is like saying "Darn, it sucks that you're down there." Empathy, on the other hand, is going down into the ditch and saying "Wow, I get how you're feeling down here." Empathy allows you to appreciate the feelings and thoughts of others. Sometimes showing that you care about someone is the easiest way to raise them up. Try this the next time someone expresses how they are feeling to you. I coined it while coaching a teen in the area of personal development a few years ago. I call it the A-3 approach:

- **A is for ASK.** People simply want to know if someone cares about them. Asking a question such as "You seem like you are down. Is everything okay?" goes a long way.

- **A is for ACKNOWLEDGE.** Be compassionate with your answer. Remember that phrases such as "It sounds like you are feeling…" or "Are you saying that…?" show that you are interested in helping.
- **A is for ASSISTANCE.** It's tempting to give answers and tell people what they "should" do, think or say. However, it's better to simply ask "Can I help in any way?" This gives the person the option to tell you how you can be a good friend.

#2 – Is there someone in your life who has added value to you? A tutor who helped you pass a test? A friend who listened when you were going through a difficult time? A teacher or mentor who helped or guided you? Do this: take out your phone. NOW.

Is it out yet? I'll wait….

Okay, once you have it out, send a text message to that person. Tell them that you appreciate them and SPECIFICALLY how they helped you. A thank-you goes a long way to making people feel noticed and appreciated.

#3 – Write down five things you could do that would be appreciated by someone. They don't have to be major, just small ways someone would feel cared for or some type of help that they might need. Now think of a way to do just ONE of those things this week. When it comes to caring about others, nothing is too small or insignificant. Everything matters.

PHRASES TO REMEMBER

The Moonlight Rule – Use your light to help someone else shine bright.

The Pay It Forward Rule – When you add value, YOU feel valuable.

The Empathy Rule – Sometimes lending an ear is all it takes to show you care.

Chapter 8

Remove Toxic Influences

You are the average of the five people you spend the most time with.

– *Jim Rohn*

THE POWER OF ASSOCIATION

In school, I was never much of an athlete. I dabbled a bit by making my middle-school volleyball team, but not much more than that. What's strange, however, is that not only did I have athletic tendencies – I was a fast runner, lean, and a good height for most sports – but my high school gym teacher asked me personally to try out for the football team that he also coached. I never ended up trying out, and at my high school graduation, I never felt that I missed out on the "school athlete" experience. So why wasn't it important for me to play sports in school? One word: association.

Some of the friends you make in school last longer than others. I had a few small groups of semi-close to close friends throughout middle and high school, and they all had one thing in common: none of them were athletes. I hung out with the kids who played dominoes and the card game euchre. (Football practice would get in the way of participating in domino tournaments in the cafeteria!) Being an athlete wasn't nearly as important as finding a good partner for euchre. I guess that made me a bit of a "nerd," even though I never thought of myself in any specific terms.

I just liked what I liked. And I never missed athletics because everyone I hung out with was doing the other stuff. The people you most closely associate with will always determine what activities you deem important. Remember that. Many people mistakenly believe that kids who vape, do other drugs, or skip school are "bad kids." I don't think so. Life has shown me that most students are good – sometimes they just associate themselves with the wrong people. The activities that I did and did not do had everything to do with the people I associated with. That's why I never considered not being an athlete as a missed opportunity – until I visited my brother in university.

Remember the "Two Cribs" story from Chapter 1? If you recall, my mother found out that my father was cheating on her and about to have a child with another woman. Well, that "other boy" grew up, and my half-brother Kojo and I would eventually form a great relationship despite the tumultuous beginning. We grew up separately, with our respective mothers, only really getting to know each other better in our late teenage and adult years. I grew up in Rexdale, a suburb of Toronto, Canada. He grew up near North York (about 45 minutes away by car) in the East end of the city. I never played any sports. He did – eventually gravitating toward football. He developed his skill and ability and would continue playing into university.

While I was studying to get a Bachelor of Commerce degree from Ryerson University in Toronto (now known as Toronto Metropolitan University), he attended Wilfrid Laurier University in Waterloo. He made the football team, was a star player, and would eventually make the All-Canadian roster, a big deal for Canadian football players! I'll never forget going to visit him and watching some of his games in Waterloo. The accolades, the crowds…and yes, the girls that flocked to him and the other players, gave me one overwhelming feeling that until that day I had never felt regarding sports: REGRET. My mind immediately snapped back to my high school gym teacher (who was also the football coach) saying, "Kwesi, you should try out for the team. I think you'd be a good player!" and my passing on that opportunity.

A part of me will always regret the fact that I didn't even try to play football (or any sport) in school. You should always test your potential – how much you can do and how far you can go – and I'll never know how great I could have been athletically. My brother would eventually be asked to visit the USA to play in the East/West Shrine Bowl (another big deal), where he met and practiced with the eventual GOAT (Greatest of All Time) Tom Brady. (I gave Brady that title…prove me wrong!)

Kojo even played in the Canadian Football League professionally before eventually becoming a teacher and school administrator. Looking back, I wonder what I could have done in my life had I said yes to that coach. But once again, the only reason I had that feeling of regret was because I spent so much time with Kojo's football teammates and at his games. The power of association. Maybe that need for trying new things and adventure led me to the total 180-degree turn I would take in my early adult years.

THE FIRST CLUB

I didn't know her back then, but my wife got her first fake ID when she was sixteen years old. She was the *last* in her group to get one. I've never had one because – yes – association. My high school friends didn't go out, they didn't drink…I guess you could say we were pretty boring. However, I never thought of us that way – those were just not things I felt like doing. That changed completely when a friend in university took me to my first nightclub – when I was twenty-one years old. Let's just say that once I walked in, I was hooked. Drinking, dancing…women! I thought, *Why did I wait so long to get into all of this?*

No matter what age you are, you tend to follow the crowd you hang out with. When I started hanging out with "clubbers," I started clubbing. When I started hanging out with my marijuana-smoking barber, I started smoking weed. And when I graduated from university and got my first real job, my co-workers introduced me to harder drugs…and yes, I went down that road too. I'm neither proud nor ashamed of the fact that I've been both drunk and high more times than I can remember. I understand association and the fact that we tend to do what those around us do. I'm still responsible for my own behavior, but I realize that accountability aside, my behavior was heavily influenced by the people I chose to associate with. In the book *What Happened to You?: Conversations on Trauma, Resilience and Healing*, Oprah Winfrey wrote, "Your past is not an excuse. But it is an explanation." I'm not making excuses for my behavior, but our associations do provide explanations for the actions we choose. By the way, in my opinion that book is a MUST read for any teacher, principal, or other educator.

Notice one word in the last sentence: "choose." You choose your associations. The crowd you surround yourself with influences you. Therefore, what you choose to do – or not do – from now on should no longer surprise you. If people around you aren't helping you grow, it's up to you to remove the toxicity from your life. This isn't always possible due to ties such as family, but what you can do is this: deliberately choose to spend time with those doing what you want to do. I discovered this rule by accident.

A NEW "SECOND HOME"

Let's not dwell on the negative. The power of association can lead to positive results too. Take my half-brother, for instance. Kojo played football both in university, and professionally for the CFL (Canadian Football League) before becoming a teacher. He has always been into health and fitness and spent some time working as a personal trainer. Growing up on opposite sides of Toronto with our separate mothers, we didn't spend much time together until we finished high school. I always admired his athletic ability and skill as a football player. Once he started to train clients at the local Goodlife fitness center, I really took notice. I had been spending a lot of hours in the gym at that time, and the idea of getting paid to hang out in a gym was amazing to me. I thought, *I can work out, help other people get in shape…and get PAID to do it? I'm in!* I immediately signed up and got certified as a Personal Trainer. Once again, the power of association – this time on the positive side.

Simply by spending more time with my brother and his teammates when I would visit them at Wilfrid Laurier University, and then at the gym with him and his co-workers a few years later, gave me new behaviors that subconsciously influenced me. I went from drinking, drugs, and partying to working out, training people, and becoming more health conscious. I'm not saying that I stopped everything right away, but the mindset shift had begun. I would eventually train people to get healthier, work at a weight-loss center, and even compete in a fitness competition myself! The gym became my second home, and healthy living has been of paramount importance to me ever since.

Who are you hanging out with? Do you engage in the same behaviors and habits that they do? It is rare that a person will have nothing in common with the people they are closest to. There's an old belief that when two people are walking together, you are either walking at *their* pace, or they are walking at yours. You get to decide who you want to walk – and associate with. Take time to think about this; it can change your life. In fact, the reason you're reading this book is because of the power of good influences.

WHY YOU'RE READING THIS BOOK

I released my first book, *RISE: The 8 Keys to Overcoming Adversity* in November 2019. I remember some of my long-time friends showing up to my book launch. What really stuck with me is a comment I heard from most of them: "Wow, you're the ONLY author I know!" The comment struck me because I know many authors who are also personal friends. While I was proud of myself for releasing my first book, I didn't really think of myself as special or anything, because I was simply doing what many of my public-speaking friends had already done. However, it was my friend Ven who clarified this concept for me.

As mentioned in Chapter 1, I joined Toastmasters International in 2013. When I joined, I simply wanted to feel more confident as a communicator. I had no idea that I would win multiple awards and a District Championship along the way. I couldn't have imagined that I'd connect with amazing speakers and get certified to coach people to write speeches and speak effectively. And not in my wildest dreams did I think I would become a professional speaker just a few years after timidly walking into that first meeting.

It was at a meeting in downtown Toronto that I met my friend Ven. Ven is an amazingly engaging (and hilarious) speaker and a great person in general. We were both members of Keynote Speakers Advanced Toastmasters, and many in that particular Toastmasters club were professional speakers (not typical for Toastmasters clubs). I told Ven that I had thought about possibly becoming a speaker one day, and I'll never forget his response: "Well Kwesi, you're in the right place. You need to get around those you want to be like because it normalizes the process of becoming what you want to be." One word in that statement stuck with me: *normalize*.

Normalization simply means making something seem more normal or regular. By hanging out with speakers, I made becoming a speaker seem more normal or attainable because I was in close proximity to those already doing it. On top of that, many in the group were also authors. Through this club I was introduced to people who helped me learn how to write a book outline, how to find an editor, how to design a book, how to self-publish, and how to market a book. The first chapter of my book was written before the end of that year.

Do you believe in the power of association now?

If there is ANYTHING you want to do and are not sure if you can, start associating with people AL-READY doing it. Your doubt will diminish, you'll build your belief, and your connections will give you clarity and confidence.

The best thing you can do when you want to accomplish something is to get around those who have *already* accomplished it. Why do you think many professional athletes have professional athletes for parents? Ever seen an actors' son or daughter get into the same business? The same goes for musicians and many other professions.

The good news is this: even if there is no one in your family doing what you want to do, you can still go out and find role models. Get in their space...and their success and knowledge will rub off on you. I can't tell you the number of meetings I paid to be in, people I took out for lunch, or groups I joined simply to get around people doing what I wanted to do. Normalization leads to success.

Now, let's figure out how to test the power of your current crowd and if they are truly a good match for you.

THE POWER OF VALUES

This chapter started with a quote from the motivational speaker Jim Rohn: "You are the average of the five people you spend the most time with." That has always stuck with me, so I dug deeper, and it turns out to be true in many areas. Studies show that we tend to make the same amount of money, share the same interests, and even have similar body types as the people we spend the most time with.

The important thing to remember is that these similarities happen at a subconscious level. We gravitate toward those who seem similar to us.

However, we can control the process of who we attract, and it is important to do so. Why? Because when you don't pay attention to who you hang out with, you are likely to end up around people closer to the current or past version of yourself, rather than those resembling the person *you want to become*.

Can you think of someone you used to call a friend who now makes you wonder, *Why did I ever hang out with them?*

The term "peer pressure" often comes about from strong personalities overwhelming weaker ones. And by weak I simply mean people who haven't decided who they want to be around. You can make that choice and take total control of your relationships. You do it through defining your values.

Values are a person's standards – what they deem important. Also known as "core values," these words or traits reflect what you believe. They are the words that drive your behavior. I like to think of them as your compass – they show you where to go, what to do...and who to associate with. They are your guiding principles in life.

It's worth taking the time to decide what these guiding principles are for you. Examples of values include Authenticity, Balance, Status, Wisdom, Service, Responsibility, Kindness, Honesty, Fairness and Growth. Values can also be a combination of words as well. For example, my values have changed over the years, and likely may shift as I get older, but at the time of this writing I have three:

- Adding Value
- Passion over Profit
- Betterment

These values have been essential for me to define because they guide my actions and decisions. For example, when I think of "adding value" as a speaker, my speechwriting process becomes easier. I start with how I want to help my audience (mainly students and police officers) to improve their lives. Only then do I fill in the stories and activities that I'll share in my presentations. It starts with the value.

I also have a certification as a World Class Speaking Coach. When potential new coaching clients book an initial call with me, they often tell me that the value received from this free call far exceeded some of the advice they have previously paid for from other coaches and programs. This is before they even spend a dollar to be coached by me. I know coaches who charge for absolutely every minute they spend with someone, even charging from the first call. I'm not judging what they choose to do, but since my core value is defined, I have given – and probably always will give – away some valuable advice for free.

When I think of "passion over profit," this also drives what I do. I've been told numerous times that there is "more money" in speaking to corporate audiences instead of speaking to elementary, high school, and university students. Maybe that's true, maybe not. However, while I do speak to some corporate audiences, my passion is helping young people build resilience and mental health, and helping first responders overcome depression. I've been lost, lonely, and hopeless as a teen, and I'm truly driven to build the confidence in young people. In addition, as a former police officer who has suffered with mental health issues, I see far too many officers who have been depressed and suicidal, and I strongly believe that my story and message make me uniquely suited to uplift those in the law enforcement profession as well. Both "markets" – schools and law enforcement agencies – traditionally pay speakers less than those who speak on the big corporate stages, but my value is passion over profit so I'll always primarily be driven by the audiences I feel I can help the most.

Finally comes the value of "betterment." When I finished university, I swore I was done reading books. However, years later, I see that there is even *more* value in reading now that school is over. Well actually, school is never over because we're always learning. That's what this value means to me. Betterment simply means the process of improving. I want to improve myself every day as much as possible. I improve my body through working out, cardiovascular exercise and yoga. I improve my mind through reading books, listening to Audible and watching educational videos. I improve my spirit through meditation, journaling and prayer. I'm nowhere near perfect, and now I realize the truth: perfect is unattainable – life is just about getting 1 percent better every day. The more you improve yourself, the better you can be for others.

Self-improvement has allowed me to be better for my family, friends, clients I coach, and audiences I speak to.

Values are important because they guide what you prioritize and do. However, they are just as important in helping you to determine what NOT to do.

ANOTHER REASON VALUES ARE IMPORTANT

Have you ever done something and felt "off" afterwards – as if you know the action doesn't fit who you are? I vividly remember trying a cigarette for the first time. I was in Acapulco, Mexico, on vacation. I was with my brother and some friends in a club, and someone passed around a lit cigarette. Being a lifelong asthmatic, breathing has always been an issue for me. I've even been hospitalized after a bad asthma attack when I was younger, so I was never even remotely tempted to weaken my lungs further by picking up a smoking habit. However, I'd had far too many drinks that night, and "everyone else was doing it" as the old cliché goes. So, I took a puff. Then another one. BIG mistake. I immediately coughed, felt dizzy, and almost threw up (I held it in thankfully!). That was the first - and last time I ever smoked a cigarette.

When I woke up the next morning, I remember thinking, Why would I try that? I have asthma, AND I love working out and feeling great! This doesn't fit who I am at all!

You might be able to guess that association is why I tried it, but what has kept me from repeating that action was my *value* of maintaining a healthy body. If you fast forward to today, that is still a value of mine, and thus I rarely even drink anymore. That is what values do for you – they remind you of toxic actions and influences that you need to avoid.

Even if you haven't defined your personal core values, your intuition will often give you a hint as to what those values might be. When you think, say, or do something that feels out of alignment with who you are, make a note of it because that is likely connected to one of your values. What does "out of alignment" feel like? Feelings such as guilt, shame, anger, or regret often provide a clue. Sometimes your spirit just nudges you away from things you need to let go of. Awareness is your best friend when it comes to aligning with your best self.

Finally in this chapter, let's talk about categorizing and choosing our associations.

FOUR TYPES OF FRIENDS

The author Gabrielle Bernstein in her book *The Universe Has Your Back* said these wise words: "The world is your classroom, and people are your assignments." We learn about our world and about ourselves through relationships. Some people are in your life by choice – whether good or bad. However, you do have a choice in the matter and can deliberately choose your associations. While I am still learning about relationships, here are the four types of friends I've had in my life that you will likely have too, and how to approach these relationships.

SOCIAL FRIENDS

Two words come to mind when I think of social friends: Hang Out and Unplug.

There are many memes, videos, and "gurus" telling you that you must rise and grind, hustle harder, and chase your dreams. While most of these are shared by well-meaning, positive people, there are times when the push to produce can be overwhelming.

How does the saying go? "All work and no play make Jack a dull boy."

Taking time to have fun and break up the serious grind of academics, building a business, or working is not only nice to do, but also necessary. You can likely think of people in your life who are perfect to do this with. These are the friends who don't talk to you about school, work, or anything serious...at least not often. When you are stressed out and want to forget your problems for a while, chances are these are the people you think of. We all need people who help us to unplug and spend some time away and have fun.

SEASONAL FRIENDS

The two words that describe these friends are: Reason and Release.

There's an old saying that some people come into our lives for a reason, a season, or a lifetime. The only problem with this is that sometimes we put people into the wrong category. Let me explain. During my time in jail, I had people who I thought were lifetime friends. I just knew they would visit and reach out to my wife for support while I was gone. Then...nothing. No support, no letters to me, and NO in-person visits. At first, I was angry and disappointed. I shouldn't have been – I simply placed those friends in the wrong category. As I wrote in my first book *RISE*: “Expectation always leads to frustration.” When we expect others to act in a certain way and put them in a category that they don’t belong in, it will certainly lead to anger and resentment. I recently read a statistic that stated that over 50 percent of people who claim so-and-so is their best friend don’t have the feeling reciprocated. In other words, ask two people if they are best friends and over half of the time one will say yes, the other will say no.

Some people are simply in your life for a reason – maybe you’re in the same class and will be friends for the semester. Perhaps you are both going through a tough breakup or other situation and are temporarily leaning on each other. Whatever the reason is, sometimes these relationships simply run their course once you don’t share that external common situation. There will be people who you have in your life for a certain duration, then you both go your separate ways.

I can assure you of two things: First, you will have seasonal AND lifetime friends as you move through this life. Second, you will occasionally put people in the wrong category. Don't stress about it; accept it and learn as some relationships remain while others fade.

STEEPED-TEA FRIENDS

The next two types of friends are ones you ought to deliberately cultivate and maintain in life. The two words that describe what I call "steeped-tea" friends are Reliability and Flexibility. When you put a tea bag in hot water, what happens? Does the bag tear? No, it stays intact because it is flexible, and releases its flavor into the cup reliably.

This type of friend works the same way. They're the person you can call at 3 AM when you're in trouble. They don't judge you; they support you. They show up when others don't. They accept you. You can talk to them about anything and ask the uncomfortable questions. For many people, the steeped-tea friend knows things about them that their parents don't know. As actor Will Ferrell said in the movie *Old School*, these friends are in the "trust tree." They have your back and are always there when you need them. Chances are likely that you are there for them in the same way. These friends are rare, so don't think you need ten or fifteen of them in your life. Most people live their whole lives and only ever have a couple of steeped-tea friends. However, this bond is so powerful, that's all you really need.

STRETCH FRIENDS

The last type of friend – the stretch friend – is probably the one you'll almost definitely have to look for. This is because most people will not give you the two words that these friends represent: Discomfort and Honesty. Most people dislike being around those who make them uncomfortable. There are those who make more money, who are smarter, more ambitious, or simply seem to do, be, and have more than you do. The average person flees from this. They don't like to be made to feel small, so instead of using the discomfort as motivation, they run and hide from growth. Don't make this mistake.

Think of envy as a mirror. Here's what I mean. I used to be envious when I saw someone who had published a book. I didn't mention it aloud, but I would do things to avoid them such as trying not to be in the same place as they were, or refraining from liking their posts so they would fall out of my algorithm, and I wouldn't see them anymore. (Yup, I'm mature! ☺). However, when I meditated on my envy, I started to realize that I wasn't envious because they were doing something I *couldn't* do; my feeling came because they were doing something I *wanted* to do. My envy was simply the inner self knowing that I needed to step into my gift of writing.

It wasn't that I wanted my author friend to fail; it was that I wanted to succeed as well! And the reason that I was specifically envious of another author – was because I was supposed to be one myself and was running away from the call to create my own book. Envy is simply a mirror. It shows you what you *can* do, not what you lack. Try to look at it that way. The feeling of wishing it was you, is just a reminder of the inner knowing that you can do, be, and have more. I've found that *the greatest antidote to envy is action*. When I feel that envy monster creeping up, I take action – creative action – towards something I want. Try it, and I guarantee the negative feelings will disappear. That's why you need some stretch friends in your life: they are growing, and when you're standing still, you'll be reminded that you need to keep growing too. Let that discomfort drive you to act.

The second benefit that stretch friends provide is the truth. They are honest enough to let you know when you are capable of more, and when you are on a path that doesn't serve you. Two quick examples: the first is my friend Bill. When I was getting ready to publish my first book, I was excited for his feedback on my cover. I thought he would love it.

After I sent over the cover my first designer created, Bill called me immediately.

His words hit me hard: "Kwesi, I don't like it. It has no personality. It's NOT you."

I had just paid hundreds of dollars for the design, and here one of my best friends was telling me to scrap it! At first, I was disappointed. But he was right. The cover did nothing to inspire me, so I knew deep down that it wouldn't be eye-catching for anyone else either. I truly respect Bill for many things, but especially for always being a friend who is honest with me – regardless of how it makes me feel. I took his advice. I scrapped the old cover, hired an amazing new cover designer (shout out to Sandro Parisotto!), an equally amazing photographer (what's up, Eden Pereira!) and the result was a cover I loved (check it out on Amazon). None of that would have happened without my stretch friend and his honesty.

Another good stretch friend in my life is Gilbert. We met at a Toastmasters meeting in 2013 and have been friends ever since. We no longer go to those meetings together, but every few months we get together for dinner and talk about everything: business, life, marriage, parenthood, and the Toronto Raptors – you know, all the important things. It's what I call our "Mastermind Dinner," and we basically help each other improve and grow. During one of those dinners, I told him I planned on starting another business. It was early in my speaking business, and my income was sporadic at best, so I told him I wanted to start this on the side for extra income. Once again, I expected him to support the idea, since he himself has started multiple "side hustles" in his life.

However, my stretch friend was honest. He gave me a one-sentence simple advice answer: "Why don't you just focus on growing your speaking business?"

I heard these words and, just as with Bill's advice, I didn't like it. I wanted him to blindly support my idea as if he had no opinion.

Have you ever done that? Shared an idea with someone with ONLY the expectation of support? These "yes people" may make you feel good, but that placating comes at a cost. You need some critical thinkers who challenge you. That's what a good stretch friend does.

I wish I had listened to Gilbert's advice at the time, but unfortunately, I've learned many lessons through experience, and this was one more. I made a five-figure investment into a side business, only to give it up less than a year later. Why? Two reasons: first, my speaking business started to grow, and secondly the business just wasn't a good fit for me. Gilbert suggested both eventual possibilities to me, and I ignored him at substantial cost to myself. Nevertheless, I'm grateful to have these types of stretch friends in my life…I just need to listen to their advice more often ☺.

As we get ready for the final, and in some ways most important, chapter, I'll leave you with this suggestion: analyze your friends. Determine where people fit in your life.

And…make sure you have a couple of stretch friends by your side.

UNBREAKABLE BLUEPRINT:

REMOVE

#1 - Make a list of your Top 3 values. Start by choosing words that stand out to you on the following page and add your own if necessary. Circle all that apply to you, then narrow the list down to your Top 9, your Top 6, then finally your Top 3. (See next page.)

Accountability	Achievement	Adaptability	Adventure	Affection
Ambition	Authenticity	Balance	Beauty	Being the Best
Change/Variety	Close Relationships	Commitment	Community	Compassion
Competition	Contribution	Cooperation	Courage	Creative Expression
Decisiveness	Diversity	Equality	Excellence	Fairness
Faith	Fame	Family	Financial Stability	Fitness
Friendship	Fun	Generosity	Growth	Health
Humor	Honesty	Humility	Independence	Inner Peace
Integrity	Involvement	Joyfulness	Justice	Kindness
Knowledge	Leadership	Learning	Legacy	Nature
Optimism	Patience	Perseverance	Personal Expression	Playfulness
Power	Privacy	Recognition	Reliability	Reputation
Respect	Responsibility	Risk-taking	Self-Discipline	Self-Expression
Simplicity	Spirituality	Sportsmanship	Stability	Success
Teamwork	Trust	Truth	Vulnerability	Wealth
Well-being	Wisdom			

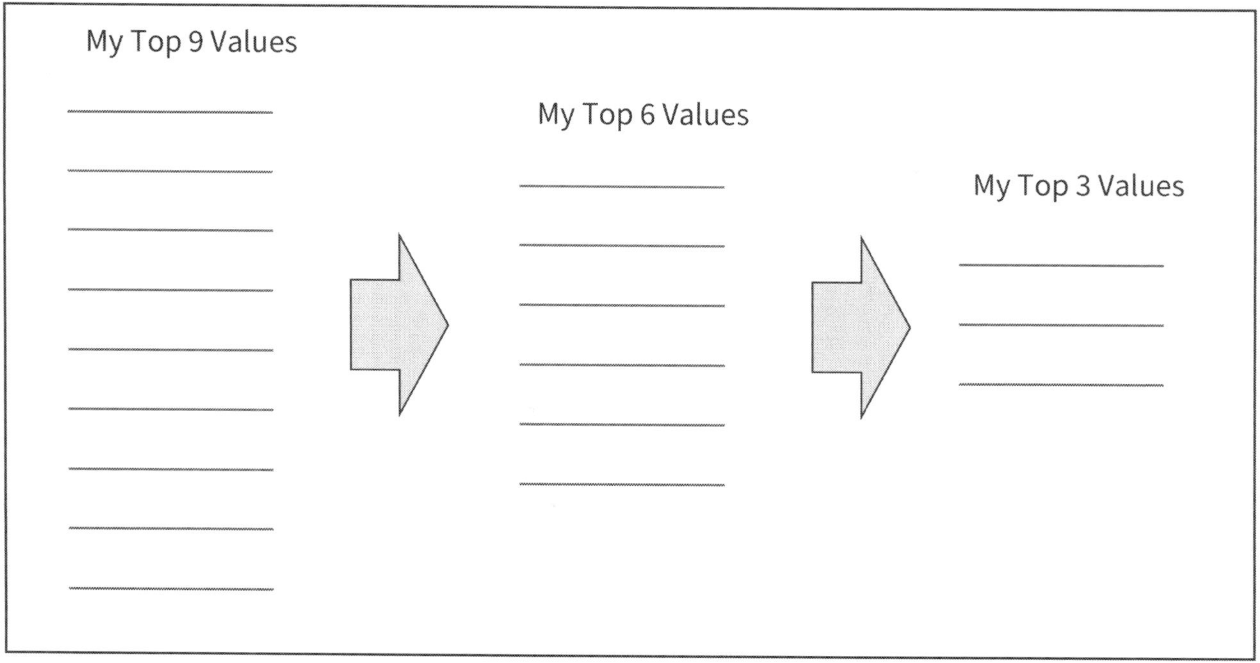
My Top 9 Values
My Top 6 Values
My Top 3 Values

#2 – Now that you have your top 3 values, do this: write down the five people that you spend the most time with. These can be family or friends, but don't just think of people in your household. Make sure you write each person's name separately (for example, don't write "parents" if you choose to use them; Mom and Dad get their own separate spots). Now write a number beside each name between 1 and 3. Write a one if that person only matches one of your top three values, two beside their name if they match two of your values, and three if they match all your top three.

Total the numbers – your highest possible score is 15, if each person in your top five matches all three of your personal core values. (You can repeat this exercise for your top 6 and 9 if you wish.) This is simply an awareness exercise. If you ended up with a low score (less than 9), it doesn't mean that you must dump your friends (or family ☺), but you may want to keep your values top of mind on a regular basis to start attracting people in your life who more closely match what you value. A good way to do this is to write your values on a Post-it note or card and keep it handy. If you like, post a pic of your value card online with the hashtag #valuescard. (Tag me in your post @KwesiSpeaks).

#3 – Is there a habit or an action that you want to stop? Here's a way to test if it is toxic: can you stop it for 30 days? The author Darren Hardy once said that if you can't stop doing something for 30 days, it may be a negative influence in your life. That's not necessarily true for everything, but it is a good test for yourself to see if there are actions that are holding you back from being your best self. Try it… and if you need an accountability partner, reach out for help.

PHRASES TO REMEMBER

The Association Rule – Your community is your compass.

The Shared Sunlight Rule – Surround yourself with stars and you will shine.

The Habit Rule – What you do becomes who you are.

Chapter 9

Reserve Silent Time & Space

The present moment is the field on which the game of life happens. It cannot happen anywhere else.

– *Eckhart Tolle*

YESTERDAYS & TOMORROWS

The future is a fictional term. All that exists is the present moment to come. In school, I was always hovering between two feelings – regret over what I wished I had done differently, and apprehension over what was to come. Whether it was something dumb that I had said, or a test that I was dreading, I was always living in either yesterday or tomorrow. Regret and worry – those are the states in which most people live. The problem with that is that the only time in which *anyone* lives is right now – today. You can work to correct the mistakes you made yesterday; you can plan for tomorrow. But there is always, only, ever today. In prison, that became crystal clear for me.

When I walked through those doors on October 31, 2017, (yup, Halloween of all days!) I remember a few moments distinctly. The final look into my mother's and wife's eyes as that heavy metal door slammed behind me, as I said goodbye to the outside world. Surrendering my personal belongings and clothing. Submitting to the naked body search. Putting on the orange jumpsuit. And the warden's words to me: "You're a cop. There's NO way we're placing you in general population!"

You see, cops and criminals tend not to get along too well… so for my protection, I was placed in solitary confinement. For most people, solitary is reserved for punishment. For me, it was the one place where I could remain anonymous…and safe. So, there I was, sitting in a concrete cell alone for 23.5 hours per day. Well actually, for the first few days, it was a full 24 hours. The 30 minutes out of the cell was permitted to allow prisoners to take a shower and have a "yard walk" outside if desired. However, due to my fear that I might be seen by other inmates and potentially recognized, I opted to stay in my cell for those first few days. Eventually the need to feel clean again finally won over, and I took the guards up on the offer.

Obviously, days were long and repetitive, and though all was quiet, my mind was a thunderstorm with turbulent thoughts racing through it. What I realize now is that the reason for my anxiety was because I got caught up in that "yesterday" and "tomorrow" thinking. Whether it was mourning the policing career that I had lost, or worrying about what the future would hold for me professionally, I was on a mental seesaw constantly. Most people live their lives this way, jumping back and forth between past and future thoughts. The problem with this is that dwelling on the past only makes you depressed about what you can't change, and worrying about the future keeps you anxious with the anticipation of possibilities to come. At the time I didn't perceive this wisdom;

however, a book in the prison library led to a breakthrough that helped me to mentally survive my time "inside."

THE GIFT OF THE PRESENT MOMENT

Have you ever been talking to someone and could just tell they weren't there? It's almost as if they were looking right through you. Sometimes they're not even looking at you – maybe glancing at their phones or looking at other people walking by while you're talking. I don't know about you, but in those moments, I want to stop talking immediately and walk away.

On the other hand, has someone ever spoken to you and made you feel like you were the ONLY one in the room? As if you were the only person in the world that mattered at that moment? Doesn't that feel amazing? Those people have mastered the art of being completely present in the conversation. It's almost magical when you live completely in the moment. In that solitary cell, I found a book called

A New Earth by Eckhart Tolle that reminded me of the power of presence.

The only reason that I picked up that book with the torn-off cover from the lowest shelf of that little prison library is because I recognized the author. I had read Tolle's previous book, *The Power of Now*, a few years before. To be honest, I didn't like it when I first read it. The concepts went over my head, and the book was just a hard read. However, beggars can't be choosers, and the selection process in jail was not like walking into a Chapters/Indigo! No lovely sections separated by topic, and definitely no aroma of Starbucks as I looked through the titles available. So, I took the book back to my cell and sat down to read it. I'm so glad I did. I may not have liked *The Power of Now* (I've since re-read it and appreciate it more now), but *A New Earth* has become one of my very favorite books. Here are the best quotes from the book from my perspective, and why I gained so much from them as I read.

The primary cause of unhappiness is never the situation but your thoughts about it.

Being in a prison cell was my situation. I always thought that the physical situation I was in was what made me unhappy. This quote reminded me that it is always our thoughts that create our feelings, rarely the external situation alone. It is not always easy to do, but when you ask yourself, *What do I think about this situation?*, chances are it's the internal thought, not necessarily the external reality, that has caused whatever negative feeling you are experiencing. This made me realize that I could become happier (or at least less unhappy) by simply changing my thinking.

You can only lose something that you have, but you cannot lose something that you are.

On December 12, 2017, I was visited by three officers in the RCMP. Papers were slid across the desk in the warden's office to me. The message was clear: "Your services are no longer required." That was the day that I was fired by the RCMP. Police officers often find it difficult to identify themselves outside of their careers. They live and breathe the profession, and when it is gone, many do not cope very well. There's a reason that many retired first responders suffer with depression – they spent so much time in uniform that they don't know who they are when they take it off. I thought that if I wasn't a police officer, I didn't have any value to add to the world. This quote helped me see that policing was something that I did for a living – it wasn't my life. Whether it's a profession, a sport you play, or a title you've earned, remember that those are external things that can be taken away. Who you are underneath cannot be lost. Hang on to that.

Acknowledging the good that you already have in your life is the foundation for all abundance.

Remember the ChapStick in Solitary story from Chapter 5? That situation is the perfect illustration of this quote. When you choose to be grateful for the good that is in your life, you open the door for more good things to enter. The ChapStick reminded me that we can celebrate small wins, even when it looks as though we may be losing. The spirit of gratitude and celebration for what you have not only makes you happier, but it allows more good things to flow into your life. My daily gratitude practice began within those prison walls and continues to this day. Saying (and *feeling*) the word "thanks" every day will change your life.

Life will give you whatever experience is most helpful for the evolution of your consciousness.

This one was tough for me to accept initially. I couldn't imagine how being in jail was "helpful for the evolution of my consciousness." To be honest, I still do not completely understand what that phrase means. However, I take Tolle's quote to mean that whatever you are going through in the moment is what you *need* to go through in order to grow as a person.

That's why I've coined the phrase: *Grow through what you go through*. I use it in some of my speeches and have even put it on one of my company T-shirts! There are times in life that will be painful and defy understanding. During those moments, don't try to pretend everything is fine – that is not realistic. One of the best ways I've found to turn a hurtful experience into a helpful one is to ask yourself this question: "Is there a *possibility of positivity* in this situation?" By switching to this mindset, I went from a depressed inmate in prison to a productive person who added value to almost one hundred other inmates through tutoring, assistance with obtaining parole, mindset strategies, and even health and wellness tips. Through the painful experience of prison, I was able to find purpose. In the same way, you can find purpose in the midst of your pain as well.

The present moment is the field on which the game of life happens. It cannot happen anywhere else.

This is my favorite quote in the book. Simply said, it's a life-changing realization. The path to peace is truly being present. Yesterday is history and tomorrow is a mystery. Anytime you bring yourself back to the present moment, you become more focused and I promise you'll also reduce your stress. An NBA All-Star reminded me of another benefit of staying in the present moment.

THE GREEK FREAK

Giannis Antetokounmpo (pronounced *'yaa-nuhs aan-tuh-tuh-koom-pow'*) is a National Basketball Association All-Star and champion. On July 20, 2021, Giannis (nicknamed the "Greek Freak") tied an NBA record for the most points scored by a player in the final game of a championship series by scoring 50 points in Game 6, leading the Milwaukee Bucks to their first championship since 1971. With the recent dominance of two other NBA stars, LeBron James and Stephen Curry, many looked at a new star rising as a refreshing change. (During the previous decade, ALL of the NBA finals had a team led by either LeBron James or Stephen Curry in the championship round.) As expected, various media outlets jumped to interview Giannis after the monumental victory. However, it was a two-minute clip from one online interview that continued to get the most buzz.

In the clip, Giannis spoke about how players handle the success that comes with winning at a high level. A reporter indicated that some players let their ego take over, but refreshingly Giannis had not. This is what the NBA star said in response: "When you focus on the past, that's your ego. When I focus on my future, that's my pride. I try to focus on the present, in the moment, and that's humility. That's being humble."

Staying present, in the moment, allows you to stay away from the two pitfalls of past and future thinking. You stop thinking of all the things you have done – good or bad – and you don't try to predict all the things you will do. When you practice returning to the moment and simply responding daily by answering the question: "What is my right move, right NOW?" you are calmer and more centered, more present and patient, and most importantly, more at peace. Presence is power, and I make this a focus of my morning routine. Speaking of which, allow me to share how I start my day in a way that gives me peace and focus every morning.

THE 5-S MORNING

What's the first thing you do when you wake up each day? For over 80 percent of people the answer is: "I look at my phone." Most people get caught up in other people's lives and requests before they even brush their teeth! Is it any wonder that the whole world feels like it's on a highway, rushing from sunrise to bedtime? How can you avoid that feeling? For me it's about reserving time for myself each morning.

Think about that word: reserve. This word is defined as "to arrange to be kept for the use of a particular person and not given to anyone else." One of the most common uses is when it comes to making a reservation at a restaurant. The process is simple: you call the restaurant (or book online), and a table is saved for you starting at the time you request. No one else has access to the table you reserve for the time that you book it and you can rest assured that the spot is saved just for you. We think nothing of doing that when it comes to eating, so why not reserve a "spot" in time for yourself every morning. Time that is set for you and no one else. A small space of peace and selfish solitude (yes you deserve it!) that you can use for whatever helps you start your day with positivity and energy. It can be as little as five minutes each morning, but if you can give yourself 10, 20 minutes or more that is even better. If you'd like some ideas on what to do during this time, here is what I do during my "5-S mornings" for inspiration.

THE FIRST S - SILENCE

It's no secret that we live in a noisy world. Most people know that intuitively, but when you are deliberately silent, I promise you'll realize how few and far between our quiet moments really are.

Try this: sit in ONE minute of pure silence every morning. Focus on your breathing, and don't "try" to still your mind. Just breathe. I caution you not to try to clear your mind because that is the hiccup that many people get stuck on. They think, *I can't clear my mind of thoughts so why try to be silent at all?* They treat silence as some sort of challenge they have to conquer, instead of a simple, gentle daily practice. That's all this is – *practicing* being silent. You don't have to get it "right," just give it a shot. ONE minute of silence to start your day. Making this change has been the biggest source of peace in my life.

THE SECOND S - STRETCH

Studies have shown that simply stretching for a few minutes every day releases endorphins – the feel-good hormones – in your body. But do I really need to tell you that? You know the feeling that a good stretch gives you. It also helps to improve blood flow throughout the body and improves your flexibility.

Personally, I stretch for at least ten minutes every morning. Sometimes I even combine it with the first S (silence) and make stretching a form of meditation by focusing on deep breathing while I do it. Try a set of full body stretches every morning to start your day.

THE THIRD S - SPIRIT

According to the book *Resilience: The Science of Mastering Life's Greatest Challenges* by Steven M.

Southwick and Dennis S. Charney, there are ten factors that can help anyone become more resilient when faced with the challenges of life. One of the factors listed is to turn to a religious or spiritual practice as a source of strength.

Those two words – religion and spirituality – can be a source of division and controversy for many people, so I'll simply say that for me, the belief that there is something bigger in this universe has helped me to stay strong during the storms of uncertainty in life. I meditate and pray daily, and I know these two things have allowed me to rise above the various struggles I've encountered. I don't have all the answers, so I rely on listening in silence to the "voice" of God to guide me in life.

If you're curious about the ten factors listed in the book, the authors found that the people who had the greatest resilience do the following.

1. Confront their fears.
2. Maintain an optimistic yet realistic outlook.
3. Seek and accept support from others.

4. Imitate strong role models.
5. Develop and live by a moral code, a.k.a. values.
6. Turn to a religious or spiritual practice.
7. Take care of their physical and emotional health.
8. Look for meaning and opportunity in the midst of adversity.
9. Accept the things they cannot change.
10. Take responsibility for their own growth and emotional well-being.

THE FOURTH S - SCRIPT

A friend once told me: "If you stay in your head, you're dead." Strong words, but you can't achieve any clarity in your life if you never make any sense of the tornado of thoughts breezing through your mind daily. The statistics vary, but the consensus is that we think thousands of thoughts daily. When you take the time to put some of those thoughts on paper, it calms the mental chaos that leaves many people anxious and confused.

In my guided *RISE Journal*, I make it easier to write, a.k.a. script, every day by using prompting sentences as a starting point in four main areas: Gratitude, Planning, Self-Talk and Reflection. (If interested, you can check out this journal at www.kwesimillington.com/store).

I also write daily in a blank journal at various times during the day when thoughts arise. You'd be amazed at the thoughts that come out of your mind onto a page, even more so when you look back days, weeks, or even months later at the insights you've recorded.

THE FIFTH S - SWEAT

Finally, I rarely go more than a day or two without getting in a workout of some kind. Studies have proven definitively that exercise reduces anxiety, boosts mental health, and gives you more energy. If you're a student, it also provides the added benefit of improving concentration and focus. Every workout makes me feel more energized, powerful and gives me mental clarity. That's why I work out in the morning – I can't think of a better way to start the day.

So here you have some ideas of what you can do in the morning for your "me time." You have the "what," now here's the "why." So much of our lives is absorbed into the lives of others. I used to wake up in the morning, look at what other people were doing, saying, or advising, and one of my first thoughts of each day would be, *What am I NOT doing enough of?*

I would wake up feeling inferior and insecure, immediately hopping on the hopeless treadmill of "doing." I was hoping that if I did this or that, then I would be enough. Fit enough, smart enough, popular enough… add your own "enough" to this list. My 5-S mornings aren't just a great way to start a day – it's my mental medication for a positive sense of self-worth and a feeling of "enoughness." Whatever you choose to do to start your day, make it YOUR time. Be selfish with your mornings, and your day – and life – will be so much more satisfying and meaningful.

WHAT DO YOU LOVE TO DO?

I'll end this chapter with one of my favorite quotes. It's a quote I use at the end of my speeches when talking to students. It's from the American author Howard Thurman:

Don't ask yourself what the world needs. Ask yourself what makes you come alive and go do that, because what the world needs is people who have come alive.

There is so much pressure on young people today. If you're growing up in this time, you must feel like the only way to matter is to be a sexy, slim, millionaire with a million followers online. In the pursuit of the perfect career, the perfect body, and the perfect selfie, most people have lost the ability to correctly identify what truly brings them joy. The voices of other people – some of whom we don't even know – have become the drivers of our lives. I'm not saying that you should ignore the advice you receive. Just make sure you don't lose the ability to hear the voice of intuition and insight that comes from your heart, mind and soul.

I remember speaking at a youth conference in Dallas, Texas. I referred to Thurman's quote to end my speech, and afterwards saw a student with tears in her eyes. I gave her a hug and asked why she was crying. She said that sometimes she didn't feel she had value outside of the occupation she was pursuing – becoming a doctor. After talking to her for a few minutes, I learned that she was dealing with a lot of academic and parental pressure to succeed.

Far too often, I see that: well-meaning parents pushing their children so hard to succeed, that they inevitably feel like failures, no matter how hard they work. That's why I love Thurman's quote so much. It's a reminder that what the world wants from you is not nearly as important as what you want for yourself. The cliché "follow your heart" is overused yes, but it's true.

If there is something you want to do – something in your heart that calls to you – do NOT ignore it. Why? Because that small voice will be with you for the rest of your life. And until you follow it, until you do what makes YOU come alive, you'll never be truly happy. Find what brings you joy, and even if it isn't what makes you money, do it whenever you can. Your heart will thank you.

So how do you find what "makes you come alive"? Use what I call the 3-C Rules to give you a clue. The 3-C Rules are the Childhood Rule, the Clock Rule, and the Curiosity Rule.

THE CHILDHOOD RULE

I once read that what we love as children, we love forever. Full disclosure – I wasn't the best student... for most of my years in school I hovered between mid-B's and strong C's in most of my courses. However, the one passion that I had from a young age was writing. My first poem was published when I was just five years old (It was in the school yearbook but I'll take it!). Growing up, English was my best class – the one I actually got a few A's in! The reason I mention that to you, is because that passion has stuck with me. I've written hundreds of poems, multiple books, and of course the speeches that I share with students and first responders. There were years that I forgot about my passion for putting pen to paper, but once I returned to it, I've never stopped.

Have you heard the oft-used phrase "Follow your passion"?

I believe it's true. However, for some the correct advice should be "Don't forget your passion." If any adult tells you that they don't know what their passion is, I think many are wrong. They have simply forgotten what they were passionate about. If there is something that you love to do, that you can do for hours on end without noticing the time – something that gives you joy – make a note of that thing...and never stop doing it. You may have to go back to your younger years to remember what it is, but digging in the treasure of your memory bank is well worth it.

THE CLOCK RULE

As I hinted to in the last section, another key to finding what gives you joy, a.k.a. "what makes you come alive," is to ignore the clock and ask yourself: "What can I do for hours (or at least a long time) without noticing that time has passed?"

Warning – not everything falls into this rule. I've spoken to students who dive down the social media rabbit hole for hours on end and pass the time scrolling and consuming content. There's a major difference between this type of "passing the clock" activity and one that deserves the label of "passion." This distinction comes down to ONE word: Feeling. How do you feel after you have watched online content (or any other habit that takes up a lot of your time) vs how do you feel after doing something you love?

What I've found to be true is that it typically comes down to creating vs consuming. When you are consuming (i.e.: simply watching and listening to content produced by others), your brain is "turned down" – you're not in a space of expansion and joy – you're simply absorbing. Of course, there is positive consumption – podcasts, motivational videos and personal development books for example. However, once again, it comes down to the feeling you get from the consumption. Do you feel inspired and motivated afterwards? Or do you just feel overwhelmed and drained. I'd suggest cutting back on the consumption that results in the latter feeling. Hey, ALL consuming has its time and place (I've been down a few rabbit holes myself this week!), but when you are creating something – writing, drawing, filming, playing music – your mind is active, you are creative, you are adding to the world. And if you are creating something you love to produce, time still passes without you noticing. Creating leads to creativity, to joy, and if you share it with the world – it can help, inspire, and motivate others.

Try this: start by adopting a 2:1 rule for consumption and creation: for every 10 minutes that you consume content, spend 5 minutes creating or immersing yourself in something that gives you joy. You may find that the joy of creating gives you more energy and may even lead to a lifelong passion.

THE CURIOSITY RULE

Finally, if you're thinking, *Kwesi, I am not passionate about ANYTHING*, I have a two-word suggestion for you: Stay Curious. Curiosity breeds resilience.

That may sound like a bold statement, but here's how the two are related. When you struggle or go through adversity, staying curious to options forces your brain to search for answers.

When faced with a problem, do you ask a curiosity question such as "How can I look at this differently?" or "How can I get through this?" Studies have shown that expansive curiosity questions help your brain to be creative and search for answers. When it comes to finding a passion, ask yourself probing questions such as "How can I spend my free time differently?" or "What can I try that I've never done before?" Such questions can open doors to new dreams and possibilities. I know this to be true from personal experience.

When I was first charged with perjury, there was a two-year gap between when I found out about the charge, and my first day of trial (the slow wheels of the justice system for ya!). I was at a low point mentally, as for the first time in years I was forced to face the possibility of no longer being a police officer. I don't know where I heard it first, but I learned that one of the best ways to build your confidence when you're feeling low is to face a fear you have. A few friends of mine had tried sky-diving, but I said a big "Hell no!" to that.

Then one day I was on YouTube watching my favorite speaker, Les Brown, deliver a speech. During his talk he mentioned Toastmasters – an organization dedicated to helping people to become better at public speaking – so I joined. Why? Because I was curious. That curiosity led me to the realization that I could succeed in a field other than law enforcement.

One speech led to another, which led to me hiring coaches and eventually becoming a speaker as well as a Certified Speech Writing Coach myself. On top of it all, I met many self-published authors during my time in Toastmasters who helped me along the way to publishing my first book *RISE*, my next two books, as well as the book you're reading right now. By staying curious and open to life, I've found a new passion, built a business as a professional speaker and coach, and even became a best-selling author (my first book *RISE* made the top 10 list on Amazon!). Stay curious. Try new things. You have a passion. And now you have the tools to discover it and bring it out. As Mark Twain once wrote: "The two most important days in your life are the day you are born, and the day you find out why." You were born on purpose, for a purpose. Go discover what brings you joy.

I believe in you.

UNBREAKABLE BLUEPRINT:

RESERVE

#1 – Start your new “presence practice” in three steps. First, choose a time of the day when you can give yourself 3-5 minutes that’s just for you. I suggest starting with a short time frame to ensure your success. (After all, who can’t give themselves 3 to 5 minutes a day?) Second, decide what activity you will do during that time. Make it electronic-free (no phones!), silent, and away from distraction.

For your first activity, I suggest simply closing your eyes and counting breaths to bring yourself back to presence. However, some people I know like to do some deep stretches, or even go for a walk (for longer silent reflection times). Finally, note the thoughts that came from your practice of silence in your journal. The path to peace is presence, so dedicate some time that’s just for you.

#2 – Write down two phrases in a notebook: “I admire” and “I accept.” Under “I admire,” write down three positive things you like about yourself. Under “I accept,” write down three things that you may not love about yourself but can accept. An example might be: “I accept that I make impulsive decisions at times.” Writing this statement helps you to realize that while you may want to work on changing some of these traits or personal descriptions, you are not going to keep beating yourself up for them.

#3 – Find what makes you feel alive, a passion of yours, and set aside time every week to do more of it. Do you enjoy reading? Set aside time to read more. Like to play music? Set aside time to play more. Enjoy putting pen to paper? Write more. The world needs more people who spend time in their areas of personal joy. Turn off the screens and do more of what you love.

PHRASES TO REMEMBER

The Presence Rule – The path to peace is presence.

The Paradox of Time Rule – The best way not to be overwhelmed by the moment, is to return to the moment.

The Happiness Rule – Don't chase joy, choose joy.

Conclusion

Many things learned in prison. Blessed I'm still living… Dear Lord, can you hear me? Tell me what to say…

– *Tupac Shakur*

Another Letter

Tupac was one of my favorite artists. Despite his flaws and failures, the one thing you knew is that you were seeing the same Tupac whether you saw him in music videos or during interviews. He brought the same version of himself to everything that he did. Sounds simple, but few live like he did.

Every day we meet people who show the world different versions of themselves, depending on the situation they are in. They may change who they are to impress someone, to show a more positive side online, or to get something they want. We meet very few universally authentic people. I'll be honest, sometimes I have to remember this myself. I try to be myself in all situations, but I need reminders at times too.

Therefore, to close our time together, I'd like to leave you with another letter. A letter I wrote to my younger self, but truly – a letter I'm writing to YOU. A reminder that you are…

ENOUGH

The world will try to convince you that you're not.
You'll often feel as if you're not.
But you are.

Yah, I know you don't believe me. How could you?
You see the dream lives lived out as reality.
You see the perfection and the sunny destinations.
You see the admiration and attention.

And you think no one cares about you.

And as long as you dwell on that, you'll never feel as if you measure up.
You'll always be treading water, but never reaching the shore.
You'll always be running, but never see the finish line.
You'll always be reaching, but never grasping that imaginary shiny penny.
The feeling of enough.

The paradox is this. You're trying to capture what you already are.
You're trying to light a burning match.
Pour water into a full cup,
Breathe air into full lungs.

Just. STOP.

Stop trying to be.
Breathe.

You are. All you need.

My friend. Thank you for taking this journey with me. Thank you for committing to live your fullest life. Use the steps within this book to live YOUR life.

A life of joy.

A life of strength.

A life of purpose.

And if you ever need, I'm here for you. I got you. Much love ☺

Your friend,

Kwesi

kwesi@kwesimillington.com

ABOUT THE AUTHOR

Kwesi Millington is a former police officer and now an international keynote speaker and certified coach. He works with schools and high stress organizations, inspiring them to build resilience, conquer stress, and develop unbreakable mental health.

For more information or to book Kwesi for speaking or coaching, visit

www.kwesimillington.com

Manufactured by Amazon.ca
Bolton, ON

41018616R00149